The Kinetic Sculptor's Playground

Breathing Life into Metal and Wood Through Movement and Balance

Phoenix Sterling

Table of Contents

1 Chapter 1: Foundations of Kinetic Art

Kinetic art is more than just static forms; it breathes life into materials, transforming them into dynamic expressions of motion and balance. This chapter will equip you with the foundational knowledge you need to begin exploring this fascinating art form. We'll delve into the core principles governing kinetic art, examining the interplay of balance and motion, and exploring the tools and materials you'll need to bring your own kinetic creations to life. Finally, we will discuss essential workshop safety procedures, ensuring you can explore this exciting field with confidence and care.

Balance is the cornerstone of any successful kinetic sculpture. It's the delicate equilibrium that allows a piece to move and interact with its environment without toppling over. Consider a simple mobile: the careful distribution of weight across its arms, each element counteracting the others, creates a harmonious dance of shifting forms. This principle extends to more complex kinetic sculptures, where counterweights, levers, and carefully positioned fulcrums orchestrate intricate movements. Understanding balance isn't just about achieving stability; it's about harnessing the potential energy within a system, transforming it into captivating kinetic energy.

Motion, the other fundamental element, is what truly sets kinetic art apart. Think about the mesmerizing sweep of a Calder mobile, the gentle rocking of a rocking chair, or the rhythmic swing of a pendulum. These different types of motion – linear, rotational, oscillating – each contribute a unique visual and emotional impact. Linear motion suggests direction and purpose, while rotational movement implies a cyclical, repetitive energy. Oscillation, on the other hand, can evoke a sense of calmness and predictability. By understanding these different forms of motion and how they interact, you can begin to choreograph the movements of your own sculptures, telling stories through dynamic interplay.

Now, let's delve into the practicalities. Building kinetic sculptures requires a specific set of tools and materials. A well-equipped workshop will include metalworking tools like welders, grinders, and cutting torches for shaping steel and aluminum. Woodworking tools such as saws, chisels, and sanders are essential for crafting kinetic pieces from wood. Measuring tools, including rulers, calipers, and levels, ensure precise construction and balanced designs. Remember, the quality of your tools directly impacts the quality of your work. Investing in durable, reliable equipment will pay dividends in the long run. Beyond tools, the materials themselves are crucial. Choosing the right metal or wood type for your project is paramount. Steel offers strength and durability, while aluminum provides lightweight versatility. Different woods possess unique properties – some are strong and rigid, others flexible and pliable. Understanding these characteristics will inform your material choices and ultimately shape the final form and movement of your sculpture.

Safety in the workshop is non-negotiable. Working with power tools and potentially hazardous materials requires constant vigilance and adherence to safety protocols. Always wear appropriate personal protective equipment (PPE), including safety glasses, gloves, and a respirator when necessary. Ensure your workspace is well-ventilated, especially when welding or working with finishes. Understand the safe operation of each tool before using it, and never take shortcuts. A safe workshop is a productive workshop, allowing you to focus on the creative process without the distraction of potential hazards. Proper disposal of materials, particularly chemicals and metal shavings, is also crucial for maintaining a safe and environmentally responsible workspace. Regularly inspect your tools for damage and maintain them properly to prevent accidents.

Mastering these foundational elements - balance, motion, materials, tools, and safety - lays a solid groundwork for your journey into kinetic sculpture. These are the building blocks upon which you will construct your dynamic creations. As you progress, you'll delve deeper into the nuances of each element, experimenting with different techniques and materials to discover your own unique artistic voice. Embrace the challenge, explore the possibilities, and let your imagination guide you as you bring metal and wood to life through the magic of kinetic art. Remember, the most compelling kinetic sculptures are those that seamlessly blend technical precision with artistic vision, resulting in works that not only move but also evoke emotion and spark wonder.

1.1 Exploring Balance and Motion

Understanding balance and motion is fundamental to creating successful kinetic sculptures. These two concepts are intertwined, a constant dance between stability and dynamism. Think of it like a carefully choreographed performance: without balance, your sculpture collapses; without motion, it remains static, lacking the vital energy that defines kinetic art. This chapter will explore the core principles of these interacting forces, providing a solid foundation for your artistic journey.

Balance in kinetic sculpture isn't simply about keeping the piece upright. It's about managing weight distribution and creating a sense of equilibrium, even within a dynamic, moving system. Consider a mobile: its delicate balance relies on precise placement of components, counteracting each other's weights and creating a constant shifting equilibrium. This careful counterpoise allows for fluid, graceful movement, transforming simple materials into a mesmerizing dance of form and balance. Even in sculptures that utilize motorized movement, understanding balance is paramount. A poorly balanced motorized piece will vibrate, wobble, or even topple, detracting from the intended artistic expression.

Motion, the second crucial element, introduces the element of time and transformation. It's the breath of life that animates your creation, turning a static object into a dynamic experience. Motion can be subtle, a gentle sway or rotation, or it can be dramatic, a complex series of interconnected movements. The type of motion you choose will significantly impact the overall feel and meaning of your work. A slow, deliberate rocking motion might evoke tranquility, while rapid, erratic movements could convey energy or chaos. The possibilities are endless, limited only by your imagination and the physical constraints of your materials.

Consider the different types of motion you might employ: linear, rotational, oscillating, or a combination thereof. Linear motion involves movement along a straight path, while rotational motion occurs around an axis. Oscillating motion is repetitive back-and-forth movement, like a pendulum. Each type of motion conveys a distinct visual rhythm and feeling. Experimenting with different motion types will allow you to discover which best expresses your artistic vision.

The interplay between balance and motion is what truly brings a kinetic sculpture to life. Imagine a wind-driven sculpture: the force of the wind initiates movement, but the sculpture's balanced design dictates how it responds to that force. The interaction between the external force and the internal balance creates a unique and unpredictable choreography. This interplay is where the magic of kinetic art resides. It's the point where physics meets artistry, where calculated design gives rise to spontaneous expression.

To begin exploring these concepts practically, start with simple exercises. Try balancing various objects on top of each other, experimenting with different materials and weights. Observe how the center of gravity shifts as you add or remove elements. Build a simple mobile using wire and found objects, focusing on achieving balance and introducing subtle movement. These hands-on experiments will provide valuable insights into the principles of balance and motion, laying a solid foundation for more complex projects.

As you progress, consider the relationship between form and movement. How does the shape of your sculpture affect its motion, and vice versa? A long, slender piece will move differently than a compact, dense one. The distribution of weight within the sculpture also influences its movement. By understanding these relationships, you can begin to design sculptures that move in specific and intentional ways.

Observing the natural world can be a rich source of inspiration. Watch how leaves flutter in the wind, how water flows over rocks, or how birds soar through the air. These natural movements can provide a wealth of ideas for your own kinetic creations. Consider the forces that drive these movements – wind, gravity, water currents – and how you might harness similar forces in your artwork.

Finally, remember that the exploration of balance and motion is an ongoing process. As you gain experience, you'll develop a deeper understanding of these fundamental principles and how to apply them to your work. Embrace experimentation, don't be afraid to push boundaries, and allow your creativity to guide you. The kinetic sculptor's playground is a place of endless possibilities, waiting to be explored. Each successful balance, each graceful movement, is a testament to your growing mastery of this dynamic art form. Embrace the challenge, and let your creativity take flight.

1.2 Tools and Materials

A kinetic sculptor's workshop necessitates a carefully curated collection of tools and materials, each playing a crucial role in transforming static forms into dynamic expressions. Beginners might feel overwhelmed by the array of options available, but building a functional and effective workspace doesn't require an immediate investment in every tool imaginable. Start with the essentials and gradually expand your toolkit as your skills and project demands evolve. This measured approach allows you to familiarize yourself with each tool's purpose and application, fostering a deeper understanding of its capabilities and limitations.

Essential hand tools form the foundation of any kinetic sculptor's practice. These include sturdy metal files, a selection of rasps for shaping wood and other materials, and a comprehensive set of pliers – needle-nose, slip-joint, and locking pliers, each serving distinct purposes. Precise measurements are critical in kinetic sculpture, demanding accurate rulers, calipers, and combination squares. A reliable set of screwdrivers, both flathead and Phillips, and a range of hammers, from lightweight ball-peen hammers to heavier sledgehammers, are indispensable for assembly and shaping. For working with metal, essential tools encompass metal shears for cutting sheet metal, a sturdy vise for securing workpieces, and a center punch for marking drill locations accurately. Remember, quality tools contribute significantly to precision and efficiency in your work, making the initial investment worthwhile.

Power tools, while not strictly necessary for all kinctic projects, can significantly enhance efficiency and open up new creative avenues. A variable-speed drill is fundamental for creating holes and driving screws, while a Dremel rotary tool offers versatile capabilities for grinding, polishing, and carving intricate details. For larger metalwork projects, an angle grinder proves invaluable for cutting and shaping metal components. A jigsaw, with its ability to make curved cuts in wood and other materials, can be incredibly useful for creating complex shapes. As with hand tools, invest in quality power tools designed for durability and precision. Prioritize safety features such as guards and safety switches.

Beyond tools, the selection of materials is equally crucial in bringing kinetic sculptures to life. Metal, renowned for its strength and durability, offers a wide range of possibilities. Steel, in its various forms, from mild steel rods to stainless steel sheets, provides a robust framework for many kinetic projects. Aluminum, lighter and more readily shaped than steel, is an excellent choice for components requiring fluidity and responsiveness to subtle forces. When working with metal, consider the specific properties of each type, like its tensile strength, malleability, and resistance to corrosion. These factors influence how the material behaves under stress and how it interacts with other components in your sculpture.

Wood, a natural and versatile material, brings warmth and organic appeal to kinetic art. Hardwoods like oak and maple offer durability and strength, while softer woods like pine and balsa are easier to carve and shape, ideal for intricate components. When selecting wood, consider its grain, density, and how it responds to changes in humidity and temperature. These factors affect the wood's stability and its susceptibility to warping or cracking over time.

Beyond traditional materials like metal and wood, consider exploring the unique properties of plastics, found objects, and even recycled materials. Acrylic sheets, available in various colors and thicknesses, can add vibrant hues and translucency to your creations. Found objects, from discarded gears to repurposed machinery parts, can introduce unexpected elements and textures, imbuing your sculptures with character and narrative. By embracing diverse materials and experimenting with their unique qualities, you can expand your artistic vocabulary and create truly original kinetic expressions.

Connecting and securing different components of your sculpture requires a diverse array of fasteners. Screws, in various sizes and head types, provide a reliable method for joining metal and wood elements. Bolts and nuts offer greater strength and stability for larger or more complex assemblies. Rivets, particularly pop rivets, are useful for permanently joining thin sheets of metal. Adhesives, like epoxy and wood glue, play a crucial role in bonding dissimilar materials and reinforcing joints. Choosing the right fastener depends on the materials being joined, the stresses the joint will experience, and the desired aesthetic of the finished piece.
Finally, consider the finishing touches that enhance your sculpture's appearance and longevity. Metal can be treated with various finishes, from paint and powder coating for color and protection to patinas for an aged or weathered look. Wood can be sealed with varnish or lacquer to protect it from moisture and enhance its natural beauty. Choosing appropriate finishes not only adds aesthetic value but also contributes to the long-term preservation of your kinetic creations. By thoughtfully selecting and applying finishes, you ensure that your artwork remains vibrant and structurally sound for years to come. With careful planning and a well-equipped workshop, you'll be well-prepared to bring your kinetic visions to life. Remember, the tools and materials you choose are extensions of your creativity, empowering you to transform raw materials into dynamic expressions of art.

1.3 Workshop Safety

A safe workshop is a productive workshop. Before even picking up a chisel or firing up a welder, establishing a safe working environment is paramount. This means meticulously organizing your tools and materials. A cluttered workspace isn't just unsightly; it's a breeding ground for accidents. Ensure everything has its designated place and that walkways are kept clear. Proper storage is not merely about tidiness; it's about preserving the integrity of your tools and materials, preventing damage and ensuring they are ready for use when needed. Think about implementing pegboards for tools, clearly labeled bins for hardware, and dedicated racks for larger materials like metal sheets or wood planks.

Personal Protective Equipment (PPE) is your first line of defense against potential hazards. This includes, but isn't limited to, safety glasses, hearing protection, dust masks, and appropriate gloves. Eye protection shields your eyes from flying debris generated by power tools or hammering. Hearing protection mitigates the long-term effects of loud machinery, while dust masks protect your lungs from airborne particles like wood dust and metal shavings. Gloves provide a barrier against sharp edges, chemicals, and splinters. Choosing the right glove for the task is crucial; leather gloves offer protection while welding, while nitrile gloves are better suited when handling finishes and adhesives. Never underestimate the importance of proper ventilation, especially when working with volatile substances like paints, solvents, or welding fumes. A well-ventilated space minimizes the risk of inhaling harmful fumes, ensuring your long-term health. Consider installing an exhaust system or, at the very least, ensuring adequate cross-ventilation.

Working with kinetic sculpture often involves moving parts and potentially hazardous machinery. Understanding the specific dangers associated with each tool is vital. Before using any power tool, familiarize yourself with its operation by reading the manufacturer's instructions thoroughly. Practice proper techniques and never operate machinery when fatigued or distracted. When working with power tools, secure workpieces firmly with clamps or vises to prevent unexpected movement. This applies to both metal and wood. Never attempt to force a tool or use it for a purpose it wasn't designed for. Respecting the limitations of your tools will significantly reduce the risk of accidents and ensure the longevity of your equipment.

Electrical safety is paramount in any workshop, especially when dealing with power tools. Regularly inspect power cords for damage and ensure all electrical outlets are properly grounded. Avoid overloading circuits and use extension cords rated for the amperage of your tools. When working with metal, particularly in welding or soldering, be mindful of electrical conductivity. Ensure your work area is dry and that you're not standing on a conductive surface. Always disconnect power tools before performing any maintenance or adjustments. Remember, electricity is invisible and unforgiving; taking precautions is essential for preventing potentially fatal shocks.

Fire safety should also be a top priority. Keep a fire extinguisher readily accessible and ensure it's rated for the types of materials you're working with – Class A for wood and paper, Class B for flammable liquids, and Class C for electrical fires. Store flammable materials like paints, thinners, and adhesives in approved containers away from heat sources and potential ignition points. Welding sparks can easily ignite flammable materials, so ensure your welding area is clear of any potential fire hazards. Have a fire escape plan and practice it regularly.

First aid knowledge is essential. Equip your workshop with a comprehensive first-aid kit and familiarize yourself with its contents. Learn basic first aid procedures for common workshop injuries like cuts, burns, and splinters. Knowing how to respond effectively in an emergency can minimize the severity of injuries and potentially save lives. Post emergency contact numbers in a visible location.

Regular maintenance of your tools and equipment is a crucial aspect of workshop safety. Sharp tools are safer than dull ones, as they require less force and are less likely to slip. Regularly sharpen chisels, knives, and drill bits. Inspect power tool blades and replace them when worn or damaged. Keeping your tools in good working order not only enhances safety but also improves the quality of your work.

Finally, cultivate a safety-conscious mindset. This means staying focused on the task at hand, anticipating potential hazards, and taking proactive steps to mitigate risks. Never rush a job, and don't be afraid to ask for help when needed. Remember, safety isn't just about protecting yourself; it's about creating a responsible and productive working environment that allows you to fully explore your creativity.

2 Chapter 2: The Language of Motion

Movement is the very essence of kinetic sculpture. It's the breath of life that transforms static forms into dynamic expressions. To truly master this art form, we must first understand the language of motion itself. This involves not just recognizing different types of movement, but also appreciating how they interact with materials, structure, and the environment. Think of movement as a vocabulary; learning its nuances allows you to create richer, more expressive kinetic art.

Consider the fundamental distinction between linear and rotational motion. Linear motion describes movement along a straight path, like a pendulum swinging back and forth or a slider gliding along a track. This type of movement often evokes a sense of order and predictability, creating a rhythmic visual experience. Imagine a series of metal rods suspended from a frame, each gently swaying in a linear path, their synchronized movement creating a mesmerizing wave-like effect. The simplicity of linear motion can be incredibly powerful, drawing the viewer's eye and creating a sense of tranquility.

Rotational motion, on the other hand, involves movement around an axis. Think of a spinning top, a whirligig catching the wind, or a gear turning within a complex mechanism. Rotational movement can introduce a sense of energy and dynamism, creating a more complex and unpredictable visual experience. Picture a series of interconnected wooden discs, each rotating at varying speeds, their interplay creating a dynamic, ever-changing pattern. This type of movement can be captivating, holding the viewer's attention as they try to decipher the patterns and relationships within the moving parts.

Beyond these basic categories, there's a spectrum of more complex movements that emerge from their combination. Imagine a helical motion, combining both rotation and linear progression, like a spinning propeller moving through the air. Or visualize an oscillating motion, a back-and-forth rotation around a central point, like a metronome keeping time. Understanding these variations expands your creative palette, enabling you to design sculptures with intricate and layered movements.

Harnessing natural forces offers a powerful way to animate kinetic sculptures, imbuing them with a sense of organic life. Gravity, the ever-present force pulling objects towards the earth, becomes a tool for creating motion. Consider a mobile, delicately balanced elements suspended in the air, responding to the subtle tug of gravity with gentle swaying and rotations. The slightest air current can set them in motion, creating an ethereal dance that reflects the invisible forces at play. Wind, another powerful natural force, can be harnessed to drive more energetic movements. Imagine a wind-powered sculpture with spinning vanes or flapping sails, its dynamic response to the wind creating a visual spectacle.

The key to working with natural forces lies in understanding their characteristics and limitations. Gravity provides a constant and predictable force, ideal for creating slow, rhythmic movements. Wind, however, is inherently variable, its strength and direction constantly shifting. This unpredictability can be a challenge, but it also presents an opportunity to create sculptures that are truly responsive to their environment. By carefully designing the shape and weight of moving elements, you can control how they react to the wind, creating movements that range from gentle oscillations to vigorous rotations.

Water, with its fluidity and inherent energy, offers yet another avenue for exploring natural forces in kinetic art. Imagine a water wheel, its rhythmic rotation powered by the flow of a stream, or a series of floating buoys that rise and fall with the tide. Water-driven sculptures can evoke a sense of tranquility or dynamism, depending on how the water interacts with the moving elements.

The environment itself can become an integral part of the kinetic experience. Consider a site-specific sculpture designed to interact with the surrounding landscape. Perhaps it's a series of wind chimes suspended from trees, their gentle melodies responding to the breeze, or a large-scale mobile that casts intricate shadows as it moves in the sunlight. By incorporating the environment into your design, you create a dynamic relationship between the sculpture and its surroundings, enhancing the overall impact of the artwork.

Remember, understanding the language of motion is not just about technical knowledge. It's about developing a sensitivity to how movement affects our perception, evokes emotions, and creates meaning. By carefully considering the type, speed, and rhythm of movement, you can imbue your kinetic sculptures with a sense of life and expression that captivates and inspires. As you explore the interplay of materials, forces, and movement, you'll discover a world of creative possibilities, transforming static forms into dynamic works of art. Experiment, observe, and refine your understanding of this language.

2.1 Linear and Rotational Movement

Movement is the heart of kinetic sculpture. It's what separates it from static forms, imbuing it with life and an engaging dynamism. This chapter breaks down the two fundamental types of motion exploited by kinetic artists: linear and rotational. Understanding these foundational concepts allows you to build a vocabulary of movement, enabling you to express complex ideas and emotions through the dynamic interplay of materials and forces.

Linear motion describes movement in a straight line. Think of a train on a track, a piston in an engine, or a simple sliding door. In kinetic sculpture, linear motion can be employed to create a sense of direction, purpose, or even aggression. Imagine a series of rods sliding in and out, creating a rhythmic pulse, or a platform extending and retracting, revealing hidden elements within the artwork. The elegance of linear motion lies in its simplicity and directness. It offers a clear path for the eye to follow, creating a sense of order and predictability amidst the often-chaotic world of moving art. You might utilize linear motion by incorporating sliding tracks, telescoping members, or even something as straightforward as a pendulum swinging in a single plane. Consider the impact of the speed and rhythm of this linear motion. A slow, deliberate glide evokes a sense of tranquility, while a rapid, jerky movement might suggest urgency or even anxiety.

Rotational movement, on the other hand, revolves around an axis. Picture a wheel turning, a top spinning, or a weather vane pivoting in the wind. Rotation introduces a cyclical element to the sculpture, suggesting repetition, continuity, and the cyclical nature of time itself. Rotating elements can also create mesmerizing visual effects, capturing and reflecting light in dynamic and ever-changing patterns. Consider the simple elegance of a mobile with delicately balanced elements rotating gently in the breeze. The rotation adds an element of unpredictability and organic movement. You can achieve rotational movement through various methods, employing bearings, axles, and strategically placed pivots. Think about using gears to connect rotating elements, creating complex interactions and rhythmic patterns of motion.

The interplay between linear and rotational movement offers rich possibilities for kinetic artists. Imagine a sculpture combining a rotating central element with linearly moving arms that extend and retract in a synchronized dance. This combination of motions creates a complex and captivating visual experience, drawing the viewer in and encouraging them to explore the dynamic relationships within the artwork. You could create a piece where a rotating disk acts as a cam, pushing a rod back and forth in a linear motion. Or perhaps a series of rotating gears drive a linear track, carrying a small object along a predetermined path. The combinations are truly endless, limited only by your imagination and ingenuity.

Understanding the mechanics behind these movements is critical. Friction, for example, plays a significant role in both linear and rotational motion. In linear systems, friction can impede smooth movement, requiring careful consideration of materials and lubrication. Similarly, in rotational systems, bearings and well-lubricated axles are crucial for ensuring smooth and consistent rotation. Consider how friction might actually enhance your design. Perhaps a slight resistance could create a desired rhythmic pulsing or a gradual slowing of movement over time. Experiment with different materials and techniques to find the perfect balance between smooth motion and controlled resistance.

Weight and balance also heavily influence the dynamics of both linear and rotational motion. A heavier object will require more force to initiate movement, whether linear or rotational. Understanding these principles is crucial for designing sculptures that move with grace and control, rather than appearing clunky or awkward. In a linear system, a carefully positioned counterweight can create a sense of effortless gliding. In a rotational system, the distribution of weight around the axis of rotation will determine the speed and stability of the spin. Consider experimenting with different weights and their placement to achieve the desired movement characteristics.

Finally, don't be afraid to explore the combination of linear and rotational movement with other forces, such as gravity, wind, or even magnetism. These natural forces can add an organic and unpredictable element to your kinetic sculptures, imbuing them with a sense of life and responsiveness to their environment. Imagine a wind-powered mobile that combines the gentle rotation of its elements with the linear swaying of hanging pendants. Or perhaps a sculpture that uses magnets to create a delicate dance of attraction and repulsion, blending linear and rotational movements in a mesmerizing display. By understanding the fundamentals of linear and rotational motion, and by exploring their interaction with other forces and mechanical principles, you can unlock the full expressive potential of kinetic sculpture and bring your metallic and wooden creations to vibrant life.

2.2 Harnessing Natural Forces

Kinetic sculpture, by its very nature, engages with the forces that shape our physical world. Gravity, wind, and even water currents can be harnessed to imbue artwork with life and dynamism. This chapter will explore how these natural forces can be incorporated into your kinetic creations, transforming static forms into expressions of movement and energy. Understanding these forces is key to creating sculptures that interact with their environment in compelling ways.

Gravity is the most constant force we experience. It's the invisible pull that keeps our feet on the ground and dictates the trajectory of a falling object. In kinetic sculpture, gravity can be used to create tension, drive pendulums, and generate rotational movement. Consider the simple elegance of a hanging mobile, where carefully balanced elements respond to gravity's constant pull, creating a delicate dance of shifting forms. Manipulating the center of gravity within individual components and across the entire structure is crucial for achieving desired movement and balance. The weight and placement of each element directly influence the overall motion, allowing you to orchestrate complex interactions with minimal intervention.

Wind, another readily available force, introduces an element of unpredictability and organic movement. Think of wind chimes, their gentle melodies a direct response to the air currents flowing around them. In kinetic sculpture, wind can be captured by sails, vanes, or propellers, transforming its unseen energy into visible motion. The size, shape, and angle of these elements determine how they interact with wind. A large, flat surface will catch the wind more dramatically than a small, curved one, producing a more forceful rotation or swing. Exploring these variations allows for a wide range of kinetic responses, from subtle oscillations to powerful, sweeping movements.

Water, although less commonly used, offers a unique set of possibilities for kinetic artists. The fluidity and buoyancy of water create a dynamic environment for sculptures, allowing for floating elements and wave-driven motion. Imagine a floating sculpture that rises and falls with the tide, or a water wheel that spins gracefully as water flows over its paddles. The inherent resistance of water can be harnessed to dampen movements, creating a slow, meditative quality, or its flow can be channeled to drive intricate mechanisms. Working with water requires careful consideration of materials and construction techniques to ensure durability and prevent corrosion.

Beyond these primary forces, other natural phenomena can be incorporated into kinetic work. Temperature changes, for instance, can be used to trigger movement through the expansion and contraction of different materials. Solar energy can be harnessed to power small motors or create electrical currents that drive subtle movements. Even magnetic fields can be employed to create repelling and attracting forces within a sculpture.

The key to successfully harnessing natural forces lies in understanding their properties and limitations. Careful observation and experimentation are essential. Start with simple experiments. Observe how different shapes react to wind or how varying weights affect the swing of a pendulum. Document your findings and use them to inform your designs. Consider the environment where your sculpture will be displayed. Will it be exposed to wind and rain, or housed in a controlled indoor space? These factors will influence your material choices and the types of motion you can achieve.

As you progress, consider the interplay between different forces. Perhaps a sculpture combines the gentle rocking motion induced by gravity with the unpredictable influence of wind, creating a complex and ever-changing dance. Or perhaps water currents interact with strategically placed magnets, producing a subtle interplay of attraction and repulsion. The possibilities are limited only by your imagination and your understanding of the forces at play. By embracing these natural forces, you can imbue your kinetic sculptures with a vitality and dynamism that captures the very essence of movement and life. This interaction with the environment not only adds a layer of complexity to the artwork but also invites viewers to engage with the natural world in a new and meaningful way. Through careful observation, experimentation, and a deep understanding of these forces, you can transform simple materials into dynamic expressions of energy and motion, creating sculptures that truly breathe life into metal and wood. Remember, the beauty of kinetic art lies not only in the movement itself, but also in the elegant interplay between the sculpture and the forces that animate it.

3 Chapter 3: Metal as a Dynamic Medium

Metal's inherent strength and malleability make it an ideal medium for kinetic sculpture. Think of the possibilities: a rigid framework supporting delicately balanced elements, or perhaps sleek, polished surfaces reflecting light as they shift and rotate. This chapter will delve into the practicalities of working with metal, focusing on steel and aluminum, two commonly used materials in kinetic art. We'll examine their distinct properties, explore various joining techniques, discuss finishing processes, and finally, consider the exciting world of mobile construction.

Steel, with its impressive tensile strength, provides a robust skeleton for larger kinetic sculptures. Its ability to withstand stress and strain makes it suitable for supporting substantial weight and enduring repetitive movement. However, this strength also means steel requires specialized tools for cutting and shaping. Consider a sturdy metal-cutting bandsaw or an angle grinder with cutting discs for larger pieces, while hacksaws and metal files prove invaluable for finer work and intricate detailing. Remember, safety is paramount when working with these tools; appropriate eye protection, gloves, and a well-ventilated workspace are essential.

Aluminum, lighter than steel yet still remarkably strong, presents a compelling alternative for kinetic projects. Its lower density allows for larger, more ethereal forms without compromising structural integrity. Furthermore, aluminum's natural resistance to corrosion reduces the need for extensive protective finishes, making it an attractive choice for outdoor installations. While aluminum can be welded, it's often easier to work with using rivets, bolts, and other mechanical fasteners, opening up opportunities for deconstructable and easily transportable sculptures.

Joining metal components securely is critical for the longevity and safety of your kinetic creations. Welding, while offering exceptionally strong joints, demands specialized equipment and expertise. However, simpler methods, such as riveting and bolting, provide readily accessible and effective alternatives, especially when working with aluminum. Crimping and folding techniques can also be employed to join thinner sheet metal, allowing for seamless connections and fluid lines. Experiment with different joining techniques to discover which best suits your project's specific needs and your personal skillset.

The finish you choose for your metal sculpture plays a vital role, impacting both its aesthetic appeal and its resistance to the elements. A polished surface reflects light, adding an element of dynamism to the piece as it moves. Alternatively, a patina, achieved through chemical treatments or natural weathering, can create a rich, textured surface, evoking a sense of age and history. For outdoor sculptures, consider applying a durable, weather-resistant sealant to protect against corrosion and prolong the life of your artwork. Powder coating offers another robust option, providing a chip-resistant finish in a wide array of colors.

Mobiles, quintessential examples of kinetic art, beautifully illustrate the interplay of balance, movement, and material. Constructing a mobile involves careful consideration of weight distribution and the dynamic interplay of its components. Start by experimenting with simple wire forms and lightweight materials, gradually increasing complexity as you gain experience. Observe how even subtle air currents animate the delicate balance of your creation, bringing it to life with gentle rotations and oscillations. As you progress, explore incorporating more intricate elements and incorporating counterbalances to achieve desired movements and visual effects.

Experimenting with different metal gauges and lengths will allow you to discover how these variables affect the mobile's overall balance and responsiveness. Consider the visual impact of varying shapes and sizes, exploring how they interact with light and shadow as the mobile moves. Remember, the beauty of a mobile lies not just in its individual components, but in the harmonious choreography of their movement, creating a mesmerizing dance of form and balance.

Incorporating found objects into your metalwork can add another layer of intrigue and meaning to your kinetic sculptures. A rusty gear, a discarded piece of machinery, or even a simple length of chain can become an integral part of your design, imbuing the piece with a sense of history and narrative. The juxtaposition of industrial materials with the fluidity of movement can create a striking contrast, sparking conversation and inviting viewers to engage with your work on a deeper level.

Consider the environment in which your metal kinetic sculpture will reside. Will it be displayed indoors, protected from the elements, or will it grace an outdoor space, exposed to wind, rain, and sun? These environmental factors influence your choice of materials, joining techniques, and protective finishes. For outdoor installations, stainless steel offers exceptional weather resistance, while carefully chosen coatings can protect other metals from corrosion. Think about how natural forces like wind and gravity can be harnessed to animate your sculpture, adding a dimension of interaction with its surroundings.

Metal offers a rich palette of possibilities for the kinetic sculptor. From the robust strength of steel to the lightweight versatility of aluminum, these materials provide a dynamic foundation for exploring movement and balance. Experiment with different joining and finishing techniques, embrace the challenge of mobile construction, and discover the unique expressive power of metal as you bring your kinetic visions to life.

3.1 Working with Steel

Steel, with its inherent strength and malleability, offers a robust framework for exploring kinetic expression. From the subtle sway of a precisely balanced mobile to the rhythmic dance of interconnected elements, steel provides the sculptor with a material capable of embodying both power and grace. Choosing the right steel for your project is paramount. Mild steel, readily available and easily worked, is an excellent choice for beginners. Its affordability allows for experimentation, and its forgiving nature makes it ideal for learning welding and fabrication techniques. For outdoor sculptures, weathering steel, also known as Corten steel, develops a protective patina, adding a rich, rusty hue to the artwork while resisting further corrosion. Stainless steel, with its resistance to rust and sleek appearance, presents a more refined option, particularly suited for intricate designs and indoor displays.

Understanding the nuances of working with steel unlocks a world of creative possibilities. Cutting steel accurately is fundamental. A metal-cutting bandsaw offers clean, straight cuts, while an angle grinder with a cut-off wheel provides versatility for curved or intricate shapes. Plasma cutters, with their ability to slice through thick steel with precision, are a valuable addition to any metalworking shop, though they require specific safety precautions. Once cut, shaping the steel components brings your design to life. Bending and forming can be achieved through various techniques, from simple hammering and bending jigs to more sophisticated methods like using a hydraulic press or a rolling mill. Heating the steel with a torch allows for more complex curves and bends, expanding the range of achievable forms.

Joining steel components requires specific skills, but the results are undeniably strong and durable. Welding, the most common joining method, fuses pieces of steel together using heat and a filler rod. Several welding processes exist, each with its strengths and weaknesses. MIG (Metal Inert Gas) welding, relatively easy to learn, is a versatile option for many kinetic sculpture projects. TIG (Tungsten Inert Gas) welding, requiring greater skill, produces cleaner, more precise welds, ideal for intricate or delicate work. Brazing, a lower-temperature joining method, offers a good alternative for thinner gauge steel or when a less visible joint is desired. Mechanical fasteners, such as bolts, screws, and rivets, provide another option, particularly useful for creating detachable or adjustable components in your kinetic sculpture.

Once the steel components are joined, the finishing process enhances the aesthetic appeal and longevity of your creation. Grinding removes excess weld material and smooths rough edges, creating a polished look. Sandblasting, using compressed air and abrasive media, effectively removes rust, paint, or other surface imperfections, preparing the steel for further treatment. Applying a protective finish safeguards your sculpture from the elements. Paint offers a wide range of color options, while powder coating provides a durable, chip-resistant finish. For outdoor sculptures, specialized metal primers and paints designed for rust prevention are essential. Clear coat sealants can preserve the natural finish of the steel while offering protection from corrosion.

Working with steel demands patience and precision, but the rewards are immense. The inherent strength of the material allows for the creation of robust structures capable of withstanding the forces of motion and gravity. The ability to shape and join steel with accuracy enables the realization of intricate and complex designs. By understanding the specific properties of different steel types and mastering essential fabrication techniques, kinetic sculptors can harness the full potential of this dynamic medium, bringing their artistic visions to life in enduring and captivating forms. The interplay of light and shadow on the sculpted steel surfaces, combined with the rhythmic movement of the piece, creates an engaging visual experience that resonates with viewers. Whether you choose the raw, industrial aesthetic of unfinished steel or the refined elegance of polished stainless, working with this versatile material opens up a world of creative possibilities for the kinetic sculptor. The tactile nature of steel, its coolness and solidity, adds another dimension to the artwork, inviting interaction and contemplation. Exploring these qualities of steel, the artist can create kinetic sculptures that are not only visually captivating but also deeply engaging on a sensory level.

3.2 Aluminum and its Properties

Aluminum, a lightweight and versatile metal, offers unique advantages for kinetic sculptors. Its low density, approximately one-third that of steel, makes it ideal for creating moving elements that respond readily to subtle forces like air currents or gentle touch. Imagine a mobile delicately poised, its aluminum components dancing in the slightest breeze – this responsiveness is a key attribute of the metal. This characteristic is especially valuable in large-scale kinetic works where weight can become a significant engineering challenge. Aluminum's lightness minimizes stress on supporting structures and motors, allowing for more complex and ambitious designs. Think of expansive, wind-driven sculptures where aluminum's low mass allows for graceful, sweeping movements that would be impossible with heavier materials. This doesn't mean, however, that aluminum sacrifices strength for lightness.

While not as strong as steel, aluminum alloys offer sufficient strength for many kinetic applications. The 6061-T6 alloy, for instance, is commonly used in sculpture due to its favorable strength-to-weight ratio and excellent corrosion resistance. This specific alloy is favored for its ability to be easily welded and machined, allowing for intricate designs and precise construction. Consider a sculpture incorporating complex, interlocking gears – the machinability of 6061-T6 aluminum allows for the precise tolerances required for smooth, reliable operation. Furthermore, aluminum's natural oxide layer provides inherent protection against corrosion, reducing the need for elaborate protective coatings, particularly in outdoor installations. This resistance to weathering ensures the longevity of the artwork, preserving its intended form and function over time. The natural finish of aluminum also offers aesthetic appeal, ranging from a bright, silvery sheen to a more subdued, matte gray, depending on the finishing process employed.

Working with aluminum requires specific tools and techniques. Unlike steel, aluminum doesn't exhibit the telltale red glow when heated, making it more difficult to judge temperature during welding. This requires careful attention and practice to achieve clean, strong welds. Specialized welding rods and techniques, like TIG (Tungsten Inert Gas) welding, are often employed to ensure high-quality joins. TIG welding, with its precise control over heat input, allows for minimal distortion and clean, aesthetically pleasing welds, which are particularly important in visible joints of a kinetic sculpture. When cutting aluminum, blades designed specifically for non-ferrous metals should be used to prevent clogging and ensure clean cuts. These blades have a higher tooth count and a sharper cutting angle compared to blades meant for ferrous metals, minimizing burrs and material deformation.

Aluminum's malleability makes it amenable to a variety of shaping techniques, from bending and hammering to rolling and spinning. This inherent flexibility allows for the creation of curved and complex forms, expanding the sculptor's creative possibilities. Consider a kinetic sculpture incorporating flowing, organic shapes – aluminum's malleability allows these forms to be realized with relative ease. The metal can be easily formed using hand tools or specialized equipment like slip rollers and English wheels, depending on the complexity of the desired shape. For intricate designs, aluminum sheet can be cut and folded using techniques similar to origami, resulting in intricate, three-dimensional forms. This process, sometimes called metal origami or folding, can produce remarkably intricate and visually stunning structures, especially when combined with the reflective properties of the metal.

The surface of aluminum can be treated in a number of ways to enhance its appearance and protect it from the elements. Anodizing, an electrochemical process, creates a hard, protective oxide layer that is integral to the metal itself. This layer not only enhances corrosion resistance but can also be dyed in a variety of colors, adding another dimension to the artistic possibilities. Imagine a kinetic sculpture with vibrant, anodized aluminum components catching the light – the interplay of color and movement creates a dynamic and engaging visual experience. Powder coating offers another durable and attractive finish, providing a thicker, more impact-resistant coating than anodizing. Powder coating is particularly useful in situations where the sculpture might experience more wear and tear, such as in outdoor public installations. It's available in a wide range of colors and textures, allowing for a high degree of customization in the final appearance of the artwork.

Ultimately, aluminum's versatility, coupled with its unique properties, makes it a compelling material for the kinetic sculptor. From delicate mobiles to large-scale, wind-driven installations, aluminum offers a dynamic medium for bringing motion and balance to life. Its responsiveness to subtle forces, combined with its durability and aesthetic appeal, provides a fertile ground for artistic exploration and innovation. The combination of lightness, strength, and workability makes aluminum an excellent choice for both beginners and experienced kinetic artists alike. Its wide availability and relatively low cost compared to other sculptural metals further contribute to its appeal. As you explore the kinetic sculptor's playground, consider the unique possibilities that aluminum offers. Its lightweight nature, ease of fabrication, and inherent beauty make it a valuable material in the pursuit of creating dynamic and engaging works of art.

3.3 Joining Techniques

The strength and longevity of any kinetic sculpture depend heavily on the integrity of its joints. For metal, several joining methods offer varying degrees of strength, flexibility, and aesthetic appeal. Welding, perhaps the most common, fuses metals using high heat. Different welding techniques, like MIG (Metal Inert Gas), TIG (Tungsten Inert Gas), and stick welding, offer distinct advantages depending on the metal type and desired finish. MIG welding, for example, is relatively easy to learn and suitable for thicker steel pieces, making it ideal for robust frameworks. TIG welding, with its precise control, excels at joining thinner materials like aluminum and stainless steel, often preferred for delicate components and intricate designs. Stick welding, using a consumable electrode, provides versatility for outdoor repairs or projects where portability is key, but often requires more post-weld cleanup.

Riveting offers another robust method, particularly for joining sheet metal. A rivet, essentially a short metal pin, is inserted through predrilled holes and then deformed on one end, creating a permanent, mechanically sound joint. Different rivet types exist, including solid, tubular, and pop rivets, each with its specific application. Solid rivets, the strongest type, require access to both sides of the joint and a specialized tool for setting. Tubular rivets, often used in lighter applications, require access to only one side. Pop rivets, highly convenient for their ease of installation, are ideal for quick assembly and repairs. Consider the aesthetic of rivets as well. Their visible presence can add an industrial charm to certain designs.

Soldering and brazing, while not as strong as welding or riveting, provide a valuable alternative for joining smaller components or metals with lower melting points. Soldering uses a low-melting-point alloy (solder) to create a bond, while brazing utilizes a higher-melting-point filler metal (brazing rod). Both techniques require meticulous cleaning of the joining surfaces and careful application of heat to avoid damaging delicate components. Soldering is often preferred for electronics or jewelry work due to its lower heat application, while brazing is suitable for joining dissimilar metals and creating stronger bonds in metal sculptures.

Mechanical fasteners, such as screws, bolts, and nuts, offer a practical and readily adjustable solution, particularly for components that may need disassembly or maintenance. Choosing the appropriate fastener depends on the strength required and the environment in which the sculpture will be displayed. Stainless steel fasteners are crucial for outdoor installations to resist corrosion. Countersunk screws or bolts provide a flush finish, minimizing visual disruption. Thread-locking compounds prevent loosening due to vibration or movement, essential for kinetic works.

Beyond traditional fasteners, consider incorporating flexible joints using hinges, pivots, and bearings. Hinges allow for rotational movement along a fixed axis, while pivots provide a central point of rotation. Bearings, available in various types like ball bearings, roller bearings, and sleeve bearings, enable smooth, low-friction movement, essential for complex kinetic mechanisms. Choosing the correct bearing depends on the load, speed, and desired motion of the sculpture. Sealed bearings are crucial for outdoor applications to protect against dust and moisture.

Finally, adhesives play a supportive role in specific applications. Epoxy, for example, can reinforce joints or secure components in tight spaces where other methods are impractical. Specialty adhesives formulated for metal bonding offer high strength and durability, but careful surface preparation is essential for achieving a strong bond.

Consider factors such as temperature resistance and flexibility when selecting an adhesive, especially if the sculpture will be exposed to varying environmental conditions. Experimentation and testing are crucial to determine the most appropriate joining method for each unique kinetic sculpture.

3.4 Finishing and Protection

A beautifully crafted kinetic sculpture, meticulously balanced and engineered, deserves a finish that enhances its form and safeguards it against the elements. This protection isn't merely about aesthetics; it's about ensuring the longevity of your piece, allowing its dynamic movements to captivate audiences for years to come. Choosing the right finish for metal components involves considering both the visual effect you want to achieve and the level of protection required. A polished, mirror-like finish on stainless steel, for example, can dramatically amplify the interplay of light and movement, while a powder-coated finish offers a durable, weather-resistant layer of protection for outdoor installations.

Think about the environment your sculpture will inhabit. Will it be displayed indoors, shielded from the elements? Or will it grace an outdoor space, exposed to sun, wind, and rain? Indoor pieces might require a less robust finish, allowing you to focus on enhancing the natural beauty of the metal. For outdoor sculptures, however, durability is paramount. Consider finishes like powder coating, galvanization, or specialized metal paints designed to withstand harsh weather conditions. These protective layers prevent rust, corrosion, and other forms of deterioration that can compromise the structural integrity and aesthetic appeal of your artwork.

Beyond the basic protective finishes, explore patinas and other chemical treatments that can add depth and complexity to your metalwork. These techniques can create a range of colors and textures, from vibrant blues and greens to rich browns and blacks. Experiment with different patination methods on small samples before applying them to your finished sculpture. This allows you to fine-tune the process and achieve the desired effect. Remember that patinas can evolve over time, adding another layer of dynamic change to your kinetic creation. Document your patination process meticulously, including the specific chemicals and techniques used. This record will be invaluable for future maintenance or restoration.

Wood, with its organic warmth and natural beauty, presents a different set of finishing considerations. While metal often benefits from a hard, protective layer, wood finishes can range from penetrating oils that enhance the grain to durable varnishes that provide a weather-resistant shield. Oils, such as linseed or tung oil, penetrate deep into the wood fibers, nourishing and protecting them from within. They offer a natural, low-sheen finish that enhances the wood's inherent beauty while allowing it to breathe. Varnishes, on the other hand, form a protective film on the surface of the wood, providing a more robust barrier against moisture, UV damage, and scratches.

Selecting the right wood finish is a delicate balance between aesthetics and protection. Consider the species of wood you've chosen and its natural characteristics. A dense, close-grained wood like maple might benefit from a clear oil finish that showcases its subtle figure, while a more porous wood like pine might require a sealant or primer before applying a topcoat. For outdoor wooden sculptures, consider marine-grade varnishes or specialized exterior wood stains that offer superior protection against the elements. These finishes are formulated to withstand harsh weather conditions, preventing rot, mildew, and UV damage.

Regular maintenance is essential for preserving the beauty and functionality of your kinetic sculptures, regardless of the materials used. For metal pieces, inspect them regularly for signs of rust or corrosion, especially in areas exposed to the elements. Address any issues promptly to prevent further damage. For wooden components, periodic cleaning and reapplication of oil or varnish will help maintain their protective layer and prevent weathering. Keeping detailed records of the materials and finishes used in your sculptures will prove invaluable for future maintenance and restoration efforts. This documentation ensures that you can replicate the original finish and maintain the integrity of your artwork over time.

When incorporating moving parts into your sculptures, consider how the finish might affect their function. Thick coatings can interfere with the smooth operation of mechanisms, while certain finishes might be prone to chipping or flaking with repeated movement. Test the movement of your sculpture after applying the finish to ensure that it operates smoothly and that the finish doesn't impede its dynamic performance. Lubricate moving parts with appropriate lubricants, choosing those that are compatible with both the materials and the finish. This preventative maintenance will ensure that your kinetic sculpture continues to move freely and gracefully.

Finally, remember that the finishing process is an integral part of the creative journey. It's an opportunity to enhance the beauty and longevity of your work, allowing its dynamic movements to captivate audiences for years to come. Embrace experimentation, document your processes, and continue to explore new techniques and materials. By carefully considering the interplay of aesthetics, protection, and function, you can create kinetic sculptures that are not only visually stunning but also built to withstand the test of time. The careful selection and application of finishes are crucial steps in completing your kinetic sculpture, transforming it from a raw assemblage of materials into a polished, enduring work of art.

3.5 Mobile Construction

Creating mobiles involves a unique interplay between metal, balance, and air currents. Think of it as a three-dimensional dance choreographed by the slightest breeze. This chapter focuses on crafting mobiles specifically from metal, although the core principles of balance and movement apply regardless of your chosen material. Remember that understanding these fundamentals will allow you to translate these skills to other materials, opening up a world of creative possibilities.

Begin by sketching your design. Consider the overall shape, the number of elements, and how they will interact with each other. A simple mobile might consist of just a few carefully balanced elements, while more complex designs can incorporate numerous interconnected pieces. Visualize how your mobile will move. Will it gently sway, or will it twirl and spin with the slightest air current? This pre-planning stage is crucial for a successful mobile.

Material selection is the next step. Lightweight metals like aluminum are ideal for beginners due to their ease of manipulation and inherent lightness. Sheet metal can be cut into various shapes and sizes using tin snips or a jeweler's saw. Wire, readily available in different gauges, serves as the connecting element, holding the individual pieces together and allowing them to move freely. For smaller, more delicate mobiles, consider using thin, flexible wire. Heavier gauge wire provides more structural integrity for larger pieces.

Now, let's consider the actual construction process. Start by creating the individual elements of your mobile. These could be simple geometric shapes, organic forms, or even representational objects. Cut the shapes from your chosen sheet metal, ensuring smooth edges to avoid injury. If you're using found objects, clean and prepare them appropriately. Drill small holes in each piece where you'll attach the wire. The placement of these holes is critical for achieving proper balance. Experimentation is key here, as even a slight shift in the hole's position can significantly impact the final balance.

Connecting the elements requires a delicate touch. Start by attaching the lowest hanging elements to their respective wires. Use small loops or wraps to secure the pieces, ensuring they can move freely. Gradually work your way upwards, connecting each level to the next. As you add more elements, continually test the balance. Adjust the wire lengths and the placement of the connecting points as needed. This iterative process is at the heart of mobile construction, requiring patience and a keen eye for detail. Don't be afraid to make adjustments.

Balancing your mobile is the most crucial step. The goal is to create a state of equilibrium where each element hangs freely and the entire structure remains stable. This involves adjusting the lengths of the connecting wires and the weight distribution of the individual pieces. A small pair of pliers is invaluable for making these fine adjustments. Think of it as a balancing act, finding the sweet spot where everything harmonizes. One helpful tip is to hang your mobile from a temporary support, allowing you to observe its movement and make adjustments without having to hold it constantly.

Consider the aesthetic aspects of your mobile. The way light interacts with the metal surfaces can add another dimension to the piece. Explore different finishes for your metal components. A polished surface will reflect light, creating dynamic sparkles and highlights as the mobile moves. A brushed finish offers a softer, more subdued appearance. Patinas can also add color and visual interest. Experiment with different finishes to find the look that best suits your design.

As your mobile takes shape, think about the overall composition. Are the elements evenly distributed, or is there a deliberate asymmetry? Does the mobile feel visually balanced, even when it's not in motion? These aesthetic considerations are just as important as the technical aspects of construction.

Finally, once your mobile is complete, find the perfect place to hang

it. Choose a location where it can catch the air currents and dance freely. A window, a doorway, or even an outdoor space can be ideal. Consider the surrounding environment and how it will interact with your mobile. Natural light can enhance the movement and reflections of the metal, creating an ever-changing display of light and shadow.
The process of creating a metal mobile is both challenging and rewarding. It's a journey of discovery, a delicate dance between material, balance, and motion. Embrace the process, experiment with different techniques, and allow your creativity to guide you. As you gain experience, you'll develop a deeper understanding of the principles that govern mobile construction, opening up a world of possibilities for your kinetic creations.

4 Chapter 4: Wood in Kinetic Sculpture

Wood offers a unique warmth and organic appeal in kinetic sculpture, contrasting beautifully with the industrial feel of metal. Its inherent lightness allows for subtle movements and intricate designs, particularly when harnessing natural forces like wind or a gentle breeze. Understanding wood's properties, selecting the right type, and employing appropriate joinery techniques are crucial for successful kinetic wood sculptures. This knowledge empowers artists to create pieces that move gracefully and endure the test of time.

Choosing wood for kinetic sculpture goes beyond aesthetics. Each species possesses distinct characteristics that affect its suitability for movement and longevity. Balsa, for instance, is prized for its exceptional lightness, making it ideal for delicate, air-driven mobiles. Its softness, however, requires careful handling and reinforcement in structural elements. Hardwoods like maple and walnut offer greater strength and durability, lending themselves to larger, more robust sculptures. Their density allows for intricate carving and shaping, opening possibilities for complex, interconnected moving parts. Consider the intended scale, movement, and overall design when selecting your wood. A small, intricate piece might benefit from the fine grain of cherry, while a larger, weather-exposed sculpture demands the resilience of teak or cedar.

Carving and shaping wood introduces another layer of artistic expression in kinetic sculpture. Traditional hand tools, like chisels and gouges, offer precise control, allowing for intricate details and organic forms. Power carving tools, such as rotary tools and die grinders, expedite the process, especially for larger sculptures or repetitive elements. Understanding wood grain direction is paramount during carving. Working against the grain can cause splintering and weaken the structure, compromising the integrity of moving parts. Sanding, a crucial step often overlooked, refines the carved surfaces, preparing them for finishing and ensuring smooth, frictionless movement in kinetic components.

Wood, unlike metal, is a hygroscopic material, meaning it absorbs and releases moisture from the surrounding environment. This characteristic leads to expansion and contraction, a crucial consideration for joinery in kinetic sculptures. Traditional rigid joints, suitable for static woodwork, can fail under the stress of wood movement. Flexible joinery techniques are essential to accommodate these natural changes. Mortise and tenon joints, modified with slight clearances, allow for expansion and contraction while maintaining structural integrity. Using screws instead of nails provides greater flexibility and prevents splitting. Another approach involves incorporating flexible materials, like nylon cord or thin metal wire, within the joints, allowing for movement while securing the wooden elements. This consideration of wood's dynamic nature is paramount for creating durable kinetic sculptures that function smoothly over time.

Understanding the inherent anisotropy of wood–its differing properties along different axes–is essential for successful kinetic design. Wood is strongest along its grain, offering maximum resistance to bending and breakage in this direction. Exploiting this strength by aligning load-bearing elements with the grain enhances the sculpture's structural integrity, especially in dynamic components subject to repeated stress. Conversely, wood is weakest perpendicular to its grain, making it prone to splitting and cracking under pressure. Minimizing stress in this direction, especially in areas with movement, is crucial for preventing damage. This understanding of wood's directional strength informs design choices, allowing for the creation of robust and long-lasting kinetic sculptures.

Finishing not only enhances the aesthetic appeal of wood but also plays a crucial role in its preservation and functionality within a kinetic sculpture. Oils, like linseed or tung oil, penetrate the wood, enriching its natural color and providing a degree of protection against moisture fluctuations. They also enhance the smooth operation of moving parts by reducing friction. Varnishes and lacquers create a harder, more durable surface, offering greater protection against wear and tear. However, excessive build-up can hinder the movement of kinetic elements. Consider the type of wood, the environment where the sculpture will be displayed, and the desired aesthetic when selecting a finish. For outdoor sculptures, weather-resistant finishes are paramount to protect against the elements and maintain the integrity of the wood over time.

Balancing aesthetic considerations with structural integrity is a key challenge in kinetic wood sculpture. While intricate carvings and delicate components can enhance visual appeal, they can also compromise the sculpture's ability to withstand the stresses of movement. Reinforcing critical areas with strategically placed dowels or internal supports can enhance strength without sacrificing visual appeal. Similarly, choosing wood species with appropriate strength properties for different parts of the sculpture can contribute to overall stability. By carefully balancing artistic vision with structural considerations, artists can create kinetic wood sculptures that are both visually stunning and structurally sound, capable of enduring the test of time and the dynamic forces they are designed to embody. This mindful approach ensures that the sculpture remains a testament to both artistic creativity and technical mastery.

4.1 Selecting the Right Wood

Wood offers a unique warmth and organic appeal to kinetic sculptures, contrasting beautifully with the often industrial feel of metal. Choosing the right wood is paramount, as each species possesses distinct characteristics that influence its workability, durability, and overall suitability for kinetic applications. Consider the density of the wood. Denser woods like maple and walnut offer greater strength and resistance to wear, making them ideal for structural components or parts subjected to repeated stress. Lighter woods such as balsa and basswood, while less durable, are easier to carve and shape, lending themselves to intricate details and delicate components where weight is a concern. Think, too, about the wood's grain pattern. A straight, consistent grain facilitates clean cuts and smooth curves, whereas a highly figured grain, while visually appealing, can be challenging to work with, prone to splintering or chipping.

Beyond density and grain, the wood's natural flexibility and stability are crucial for kinetic sculptures. Wood is a hygroscopic material, meaning it absorbs and releases moisture from the surrounding environment. This leads to expansion and contraction, which can significantly impact the functionality and longevity of a kinetic piece. For components requiring flexibility, such as thin, curved elements or parts designed to bend, consider using wood known for its pliability, like ash or hickory. Conversely, for structural elements demanding stability, opt for woods like mahogany or cherry, known for their resistance to warping and twisting. Remember, even within a single species, individual pieces can vary significantly. Carefully inspect each board for knots, cracks, or other imperfections that could compromise its strength or workability.

The intended movement of your sculpture also plays a vital role in wood selection. A piece designed for subtle, gentle motion might benefit from the elasticity of a wood like basswood, allowing for graceful flexing and bending. For sculptures involving more robust or dynamic movement, a harder, more resilient wood like oak or maple would be a better choice. The environment where the sculpture will be displayed also influences wood selection. Outdoor installations demand wood that can withstand the elements. Naturally durable woods like cedar or redwood resist rot and insect damage, but they can be more challenging to carve. Treating less durable woods with a weather-resistant sealant can extend their lifespan outdoors, but regular maintenance is essential. Indoor sculptures have more flexibility in wood choices, but consider the humidity levels in the display environment. Excessive dryness can cause wood to crack, while excessive moisture can lead to warping or fungal growth.

Experimenting with different wood species is encouraged. Start with small-scale prototypes to test the wood's properties and its suitability for your design. This allows you to refine your techniques and make informed decisions for the final piece. Consider the aesthetic qualities of different woods. The rich, warm tones of walnut or mahogany can add a touch of elegance, while the lighter hues of maple or birch create a more airy, contemporary feel. The natural color and grain of the wood can become an integral part of the sculpture's overall aesthetic. Explore various finishing techniques to enhance the wood's natural beauty or to create unique visual effects. A clear finish preserves the natural grain and color, while stains can add depth and richness. Paints can introduce bold colors and patterns, transforming the wood into a vibrant canvas.

Think about the sourcing of your wood. Sustainably harvested lumber ensures responsible forest management and minimizes environmental impact. Reclaimed wood, salvaged from old buildings or furniture, offers a unique character and history, adding a layer of narrative to your work. Working with reclaimed wood often requires extra preparation, as it may contain nails or other metal debris. Always inspect and clean reclaimed wood thoroughly before use. Ultimately, selecting the right wood for a kinetic sculpture is a multifaceted process that requires careful consideration of the wood's properties, the sculpture's design, and the intended environment. By understanding the nuances of different wood species and their behavior, you can make informed choices that contribute to the structural integrity, aesthetic appeal, and longevity of your kinetic creations.

4.2 Carving and Shaping

The satisfying rasp of a chisel against wood, the whine of a rotary tool shaping intricate curves–these are the sounds of creation in the kinetic sculptor's workshop. In this chapter, we'll delve into the specific techniques of carving and shaping wood, transforming raw timber into dynamic components of your kinetic creations. Remember, the wood you choose is your canvas, and your tools are your brushes.

Begin by securing your wood firmly in a vise or with clamps. This is crucial for both safety and precision. A stable workpiece allows for controlled cuts and prevents dangerous slips. When working with smaller pieces, a carver's screw can provide a secure grip without marring the visible surfaces. Consider the grain direction as you plan your cuts. Carving with the grain minimizes resistance and the risk of splintering, resulting in cleaner, more predictable cuts. Carving against the grain, while sometimes necessary for specific effects, requires greater care and sharper tools.

Gouges, chisels, and rasps are your primary tools for removing material. Each tool serves a unique purpose. Gouges, with their curved blades, excel at creating concave shapes and flowing lines. Chisels, with their flat or beveled edges, are ideal for defining sharp edges, creating flat surfaces, and removing larger chunks of wood. Rasps, with their coarse teeth, are perfect for refining shapes and smoothing rough surfaces. Remember to keep your tools sharp. A dull tool requires more force, increasing the risk of losing control and causing injury.

Power carving tools, such as rotary tools with various bits and burrs, offer greater speed and versatility, especially for intricate details. They are particularly useful for creating complex curves, recesses, and undercuts that would be challenging to achieve with hand tools alone. However, power tools require careful control to avoid removing too much material or creating unwanted divots. Practice on scrap wood to develop a feel for the tool's responsiveness and cutting speed before tackling your final piece.

Beyond removing wood, shaping involves techniques that subtly alter the form without necessarily decreasing mass. Steam bending, for example, allows you to create dramatic curves and bends in wood. By applying heat and moisture, the wood fibers become pliable, allowing them to be shaped around a form or jig. Once dried and cooled, the wood retains its new shape. This technique is particularly effective for creating curved elements in kinetic sculptures, like flowing arms or supports for moving components. Lamination, another valuable technique, involves gluing thin layers of wood together to create stronger, more complex shapes. This allows you to build up curves or angles gradually, achieving forms that would be impossible to carve from a single block of wood.

The interaction of negative and positive space is crucial in kinetic sculpture. Negative space – the empty areas surrounding your carved elements – is just as important as the solid forms themselves. It contributes to the overall visual balance and flow of the piece, allowing the eye to move freely around the sculpture. Think of negative space as an integral part of your design, not just empty air. Use it to highlight the dynamic aspects of your piece, framing the moving components and drawing attention to their interplay.

As you carve and shape, continually assess the balance and weight distribution of your components. These factors directly influence the motion and stability of your final sculpture. A piece that is too heavy

on one side will not move smoothly or predictably. By carefully considering weight distribution during the carving and shaping process, you can avoid costly corrections later on. Regularly step back from your work to view it from different angles. This helps you maintain a holistic perspective on the overall form and balance. Observe how light and shadow play across the surfaces, and how the carved elements interact with each other.
Remember, carving and shaping are not merely about removing material; they are about revealing the inherent dynamism within the wood. Each cut, each curve, contributes to the final expression of movement and balance in your kinetic creation. Embrace the process of exploration and discovery. Don't be afraid to experiment with different tools and techniques. It is through this experimentation that you will discover your own unique style and develop a deeper understanding of wood as a dynamic medium for kinetic art. Explore the unique character of the wood you are working with, allowing its natural grain patterns and textures to inform your design choices. The subtle variations in color and density within a single piece of wood can add depth and visual interest to your finished sculpture.

4.3 Wood Movement and Joinery

Wood's inherent responsiveness to environmental changes presents both a challenge and an opportunity for the kinetic artist. Unlike metal, wood expands and contracts with fluctuations in humidity, a characteristic that must be carefully considered during the design and construction process. Ignoring this natural tendency can lead to cracking, warping, or even complete structural failure of your kinetic sculpture. Understanding wood movement is, therefore, paramount to creating enduring and functional pieces. This chapter will explore various joinery techniques specifically designed to accommodate this movement, ensuring the longevity and artistic integrity of your work.

Traditional woodworking joinery, while strong and aesthetically pleasing in static constructions, often proves inadequate for kinetic sculptures. Rigid joints restrict the wood's natural expansion and contraction, creating internal stresses that can ultimately compromise the piece. Therefore, we must employ joinery methods that allow for subtle shifts in the wood while maintaining structural integrity. Consider, for example, the use of slotted screw holes. By elongating the screw holes perpendicular to the direction of wood movement, we allow the wood to expand and contract freely without binding against the screws. This simple adaptation can significantly extend the lifespan of a kinetic sculpture, particularly in environments with fluctuating humidity.

Beyond slotted screw holes, several other joinery techniques cater specifically to wood movement. Loose mortise and tenon joints, for instance, provide a degree of flexibility within the joint, allowing for expansion and contraction. This technique involves creating a mortise slightly larger than the tenon, providing space for the wood to move. Furthermore, the use of flexible adhesives, specifically formulated for wood, can enhance the durability of these joints. These adhesives maintain a strong bond while allowing for slight movement, preventing stress buildup within the wood. Choosing the right adhesive is crucial; traditional wood glues can become brittle and crack under the stress of wood movement, leading to joint failure.

Another approach involves incorporating flexible elements, such as springs or rubber washers, into the joinery. These elements absorb the expansion and contraction of the wood, preventing stress from building up in the joints. This technique is particularly useful in larger sculptures where the cumulative effect of wood movement can be substantial. Imagine a large, outdoor kinetic sculpture constructed with rigid joints; the seasonal changes in humidity could cause significant stress, potentially leading to warping or cracking. By incorporating flexible elements, we can mitigate these risks and ensure the longevity of the artwork.

When designing your kinetic sculpture, carefully consider the orientation of the wood grain. Wood expands and contracts more significantly perpendicular to the grain than parallel to it. Therefore, orienting components in a way that minimizes movement in critical areas can enhance the stability and longevity of the piece. For instance, in a piece reliant on precise alignment for its movement, using quarter-sawn lumber, which exhibits greater dimensional stability, can be beneficial. Quarter-sawn lumber is cut radially from the log, resulting in a more consistent grain pattern and reduced tangential shrinkage. This specific cut minimizes warping and twisting, making it ideal for components requiring precise dimensions and stability.

The species of wood also plays a significant role in its movement. Denser woods, such as oak and maple, tend to move less than softer woods like pine or cedar. Selecting the appropriate wood for your project requires careful consideration of both its aesthetic qualities and its movement characteristics. For instance, while cedar's lightness and resistance to decay might make it appealing for outdoor sculptures, its significant movement requires meticulous attention to joinery. Conversely, the density and stability of oak make it a suitable choice for intricate mechanisms where precise movement is critical.

Understanding the interplay between wood movement and joinery is fundamental to successful kinetic sculpture. By employing appropriate techniques and selecting materials carefully, you can create enduring works of art that embrace the dynamic nature of wood, allowing it to breathe and move while maintaining structural integrity and artistic vision. Remember that each piece of wood has its own unique characteristics, and careful observation and adaptation are crucial to achieving the desired outcome. Experimentation with different joinery methods and wood species will expand your understanding and allow you to create increasingly complex and sophisticated kinetic sculptures. Through careful consideration of these principles, you can transform the inherent challenges of wood movement into opportunities for creative expression, allowing your sculptures to truly come alive.

5 Chapter 5: Balancing Act: Design Principles

Understanding balance is paramount in kinetic sculpture. It's the invisible force that dictates whether your creation will stand tall, dance gracefully, or collapse into a heap. This chapter delves into the core principles that govern balance: counterweights, levers, and the ever-important center of gravity. Mastering these concepts will empower you to design kinetic sculptures that are not only visually stunning but also structurally sound. Think of balance not as a static state but as a dynamic equilibrium, a constant interplay of forces.

Counterweights are the unsung heroes of kinetic art. They act as opposing forces, balancing the weight of other components and allowing for controlled movement. Imagine a simple mobile: a light object hangs from one end of a rod, while a heavier counterweight on the other side keeps the system in equilibrium. This principle can be scaled up to much more complex sculptures, using carefully calculated weights to offset heavier sections, allowing even large pieces to move with surprising fluidity. The material of your counterweight matters. Dense materials like lead or steel allow for smaller, less obtrusive counterweights, while lighter materials like wood or even hollow forms filled with sand might be more appropriate for certain designs. The key is to find the right balance between weight, size, and aesthetic integration.

Levers introduce another dimension to balance and movement. By manipulating the position of a fulcrum and the application of force, you can amplify or reduce movement, creating a wide range of dynamic possibilities. A long lever arm with a counterweight placed near the fulcrum can generate significant movement with minimal force, while a shorter arm can provide more control and stability. Consider how a seesaw works: shifting the fulcrum alters the balance point and the effort required to lift each side. This same principle applies to kinetic sculpture, allowing you to fine-tune the responsiveness and range of motion in your artwork. Experimenting with different lever lengths and fulcrum positions will reveal the subtle yet powerful effects they can have on your design.

The center of gravity is the anchor point of your sculpture, the point where its weight is evenly distributed in all directions. Locating and controlling the center of gravity is crucial for stability. A low center of gravity makes a sculpture more resistant to tipping, while a higher center of gravity can lead to more dynamic, albeit potentially less stable, movements. Imagine a tightrope walker using a long pole to lower their center of gravity, increasing their stability. Similarly, in kinetic sculpture, carefully distributing weight and strategically positioning components can help you achieve the desired balance. Think of the center of gravity as the fulcrum of the entire sculpture, the point around which all other forces revolve.

Determining the center of gravity can be done through experimentation. For simple shapes, it often coincides with the geometric center. However, for more complex forms, it might be necessary to suspend the sculpture from different points and observe where the plumb lines converge. This practical approach allows you to empirically find the balance point, even for intricate designs. Software tools can also be helpful in calculating the center of gravity for complex assemblies, offering greater precision in your design process.

Combining these principles opens up a world of creative possibilities.

A counterweight strategically placed on a lever arm can create a dynamic system that responds to even subtle air currents. Multiple levers interconnected with carefully positioned counterweights can generate complex, choreographed movements. Understanding how these elements interact is the key to designing kinetic sculptures that are both visually engaging and structurally sound. Imagine a mobile with multiple arms and counterweights, each element influencing the others, creating a mesmerizing dance of balance and motion.
Beyond these fundamental principles, consider the visual weight of your materials. Darker colors and denser materials appear visually heavier than lighter colors and more delicate materials. This perceived weight can influence the overall balance of your composition, even if the physical weights are evenly distributed. A dark, heavy-looking element placed high in a sculpture can create a sense of precariousness, even if it's counterbalanced correctly. Playing with these visual cues can add another layer of complexity and intrigue to your kinetic art.
As you design your kinetic sculptures, remember that balance is not merely a technical requirement; it's an integral part of the artistic expression. The interplay of forces, the delicate dance between stability and movement, is what breathes life into your creations. Embrace the challenge of balancing form and function, and your kinetic sculptures will captivate viewers with their dynamic grace and inherent beauty. Let the principles of counterweights, levers, and center of gravity guide you as you explore the fascinating world of kinetic art.

5.1 Counterweights and Levers

Harnessing the interplay between gravity and carefully positioned mass is fundamental to kinetic sculpture. Counterweights act as opposing forces, balancing the weight of a sculpture's moving elements and allowing for controlled, dynamic motion. Think of a simple seesaw: the weight of one person on one side is countered by the weight of another on the opposite side, enabling the back-and-forth rocking motion. This principle, scaled and adapted, becomes the basis for complex kinetic interactions. Consider a mobile with delicately balanced arms; each element's weight is offset by others, creating a harmonious dance of shifting equilibrium. The careful placement and calibration of counterweights dictate the overall movement and responsiveness of the piece to external forces like air currents or touch.

Levers, in their various configurations, amplify or redirect force and motion. A lever's effectiveness relies on the fulcrum, the fixed point around which it pivots. The positioning of the fulcrum relative to the applied force and the load determines the lever's mechanical advantage. A long lever arm coupled with a strategically placed fulcrum can magnify a small input force, creating significant movement at the other end. Imagine a simple lever-based mechanism where a gentle push on one end results in a dramatic sweep of a large element on the other. This principle allows for the creation of sculptures that respond to subtle environmental changes or viewer interaction with amplified, expressive movements.

Different lever classes offer distinct advantages. A first-class lever, where the fulcrum is positioned between the force and the load, is ideal for amplifying force. A second-class lever, where the load is between the fulcrum and the force, offers significant mechanical advantage, allowing for the movement of heavy elements with relatively little effort. Third-class levers, with the force applied between the fulcrum and the load, prioritize speed and range of motion over force amplification. Integrating these lever classes strategically within a kinetic sculpture opens a world of possibilities for achieving diverse and complex movements.

Calculating counterweight mass requires a clear understanding of the sculpture's design and intended movement. Begin by determining the center of gravity of each moving element. This point represents the average location of the weight distribution within that element. Next, consider the leverage involved. A longer lever arm requires a proportionally smaller counterweight to achieve balance, while a shorter lever arm needs a larger counterweight. Experimentation and iterative adjustments are essential in this process. Start with estimated counterweight values and observe the resulting movement. Fine-tune the weight and placement until the desired balance and responsiveness are achieved.

Precise fabrication and assembly are paramount for the success of counterweight and lever systems. Ensure all components are accurately sized and shaped. Secure connections are crucial to prevent slippage or unintended movement, which could disrupt the delicate balance of the sculpture. Employ appropriate fastening methods based on the materials used – welding for metal, strong adhesives or precisely fitted joinery for wood.

Beyond achieving balance, counterweights and levers can become integral elements of the sculpture's aesthetic. Consider incorporating these functional components as visible parts of the design, showcasing the mechanics that drive the movement. The rhythmic swing of a counterweight or the elegant arc of a lever arm can add visual interest and enhance the overall dynamism of the piece. Experiment with different materials and finishes for these elements, exploring how they can contribute to the sculpture's form and narrative.

When working with larger kinetic sculptures, safety becomes a critical consideration. The forces involved can be significant, and uncontrolled movement could pose a risk. Implement robust safety measures throughout the design and construction process. Securely anchor the sculpture to a stable base, ensuring it can withstand the stresses of movement and environmental factors like wind. Test all mechanisms thoroughly in a controlled environment before final installation.

Consider how natural forces can interact with your counterweight and lever systems. Wind can provide a gentle impetus for movement, while gravity's constant pull can be harnessed to create rhythmic oscillations. Incorporating these natural forces not only adds an element of unpredictability and organic movement to the sculpture, it also connects the artwork to its environment in a dynamic way.

Explore different materials for counterweights beyond traditional lead or steel. Consider using found objects, natural materials like stones, or even water-filled containers. These unconventional choices can add a unique aesthetic dimension to the sculpture while still fulfilling the functional requirement of providing counterbalance.

Finally, don't be afraid to experiment and push the boundaries of what's possible with counterweights and levers. Try combining multiple lever systems in a single sculpture, or using counterweights to create complex, cascading movements. The exploration of these principles, combined with your artistic vision, can lead to truly innovative and captivating kinetic creations.

5.2 Center of Gravity

Understanding the center of gravity is paramount in kinetic sculpture. It dictates not only the stability of a stationary piece but also the dynamic behavior of a moving one. Think of it as the anchor point around which all other forces act, the fulcrum upon which your sculpture balances and interacts with the world. Without a firm grasp of this concept, your creations may be prone to tipping, wobbling, or failing to move as intended. A deep understanding of this principle allows you to predict and control the motion of your work, transforming a simple mechanism into a captivating dance of balance and movement.

Locating the center of gravity for a simple, uniform object is relatively straightforward. Imagine a perfectly symmetrical sphere. Its center of gravity lies at its geometric center. For more complex shapes, the process becomes more intricate. Consider a sculpture composed of multiple elements, perhaps a combination of wood and metal components. Here, the center of gravity shifts depending on the weight and distribution of each individual part. A heavier element will exert a greater influence on the overall center of gravity, pulling it closer to its own center of mass.

Visualizing the center of gravity can be challenging, especially with intricate designs. One helpful technique involves suspending the object from multiple points. Imagine hanging your sculpture from a string. The imaginary line extending downwards from the point of suspension will pass through the center of gravity. By repeating this process from different points, you can triangulate the precise location where these lines intersect, pinpointing the center of gravity. This practical method can be applied to individual components as well as the assembled sculpture, offering valuable insight into its balance.

Manipulating the center of gravity is a fundamental skill for the kinetic sculptor. By strategically positioning weights and counterweights, you can control the equilibrium of your piece. Think of a mobile, a classic example of kinetic art. Its delicate balance relies on the precise placement of elements, ensuring that the center of gravity of each section aligns with its suspension point. This careful orchestration of weight distribution allows the mobile to move gracefully with even the slightest air current.

The interaction between center of gravity and the base of support is crucial for stability. The base of support is the area beneath the sculpture that encompasses all points of contact with the ground or supporting structure. For a sculpture to remain upright, its center of gravity must fall within this base of support. A wider base provides greater stability, while a narrower base makes the sculpture more susceptible to tipping. Consider the implications for a kinetic sculpture designed to sway or rock: a carefully calculated base of support, combined with a strategically placed center of gravity, allows for controlled movement without compromising stability.

As your designs become more complex, incorporating levers and pendulums, the concept of center of gravity takes on even greater significance. A lever's effectiveness depends on the relationship between the fulcrum, the effort applied, and the load being moved. The center of gravity of each component influences the forces at play, dictating the lever's mechanical advantage. Similarly, the swing of a pendulum is governed by the distribution of weight around its pivot point, its center of gravity dictating its period of oscillation. Mastering these principles allows you to fine-tune the movement of your sculptures, creating intricate and mesmerizing patterns of motion.

Incorporating moving parts further complicates the center of gravity calculations. As elements shift and rotate, the overall center of gravity of the sculpture changes dynamically. Imagine a piece with rotating arms or swinging pendulums. With each movement, the distribution of weight shifts, causing the center of gravity to relocate. This dynamic shift in balance becomes a key element in the sculpture's overall movement, driving its kinetic behavior. Understanding how these shifts occur allows you to design movement sequences with precision, choreographing a captivating dance of shifting weights and balanced forces.

Consider the impact of materials on center of gravity. Different materials have different densities, affecting the weight distribution within your sculpture. A dense material like steel will concentrate mass in a smaller volume compared to a lighter material like wood. This difference in weight distribution can significantly impact the overall center of gravity, influencing the sculpture's balance and movement. Choosing materials strategically allows you to control the weight and balance of your creations, further enhancing your ability to manipulate their kinetic behavior.

Understanding the interplay between center of gravity, materials, and movement is essential for creating successful kinetic sculptures. It's a continuous process of experimentation and refinement, demanding a keen eye for balance and a deep understanding of the forces at play.

By mastering this fundamental principle, you unlock the true potential of kinetic art, transforming static forms into dynamic expressions of movement and balance. With careful planning and execution, you can harness the power of gravity to breathe life into your metal and wood creations, transforming them into captivating works of art.

6 Chapter 6: Breathing Life into Your Creations

The magic of kinetic sculpture lies in its movement, transforming static forms into dynamic expressions. This chapter delves into the practical mechanics of imbuing your creations with that essential life force, exploring the diverse methods for controlling and animating your artwork. From simple mechanical systems to more complex motorized assemblies, we'll navigate the exciting realm of bringing motion to metal and wood.

Consider the subtle dance of a hanging mobile, gently swaying in the breeze. Its seemingly simple movement relies on carefully balanced components and strategically placed pivot points. This kind of passive motion, driven by natural forces like wind or gravity, offers an elegant solution for many kinetic sculptures. Exploiting these readily available forces requires a deep understanding of balance and leverage, principles covered extensively in Chapter 5. Building upon that knowledge, we can explore how to harness these forces to create mesmerizing oscillations and rotations, turning natural energy into artistic expression.

However, when natural forces aren't sufficient, or when a specific type of movement is desired, incorporating motors opens up a world of possibilities. Motors allow for precise control over speed, direction, and timing, enabling intricate choreographies of motion. Think of a complex kinetic sculpture with interconnected gears, cams, and linkages, all driven by a small, yet powerful motor. The rhythmic interplay of its moving parts can evoke a sense of rhythm and vitality, captivating the viewer with its mechanical ballet. Selecting the right motor for your project requires careful consideration of factors like torque, speed, and power consumption. Experimentation and careful calibration are key to achieving the desired effect, ensuring that the motor seamlessly integrates with the overall design.

Beyond the mechanisms themselves, understanding how to control the movement is crucial. Simple timers can be used to regulate on/off cycles, creating predictable patterns of motion. More sophisticated control systems, utilizing microcontrollers and sensors, allow for interactive and responsive movements. Imagine a sculpture that reacts to the presence of a viewer, altering its motion based on proximity or even external stimuli like light or sound. These interactive elements add another layer of engagement, transforming the artwork into a dynamic conversation piece.

Once your kinetic sculpture is complete and animated, the next consideration is its presentation. Installation and display are critical aspects, especially for larger pieces or those intended for public spaces. A secure and stable mounting system is paramount, ensuring the safety of both the artwork and the viewers. For outdoor installations, weatherproofing becomes a key concern. Protecting the delicate mechanisms from the elements is vital for longevity and continued functionality. Materials should be chosen with durability and resistance to corrosion in mind.

Proper documentation is also essential, both for preserving the artistic vision and for facilitating future maintenance or repairs. Detailed photographs, videos, and written descriptions of the construction process, mechanisms, and intended movement can serve as valuable resources. These records not only help in understanding the artist's intent but also provide practical guidance for any necessary upkeep or

restoration. This meticulous documentation is especially important for kinetic art in public spaces, where ongoing maintenance is necessary to ensure the continued enjoyment and appreciation of the artwork.
Preserving kinetic art for future generations presents unique challenges. Moving parts are inherently subject to wear and tear. Regular maintenance, including lubrication, cleaning, and occasional replacement of worn components, is crucial for extending the lifespan of these dynamic creations. For complex motorized sculptures, access to spare parts and technical expertise might be necessary. Establishing a clear maintenance plan, ideally in consultation with the artist, ensures that the artwork can continue to move and inspire audiences for years to come.

6.1 Mechanisms and Motion Control

The world of kinetic sculpture opens up dramatically when you introduce controlled movement. Think of it as choreography for your artwork. Instead of relying solely on gravity or wind, you gain the power to dictate the rhythm, pace, and sequence of motion, transforming a static form into a dynamic performance. This control is achieved through a variety of mechanisms, each offering unique possibilities for artistic expression. Understanding these core mechanisms is like learning the grammar of kinetic language.
Cams, for example, are incredibly versatile. These rotating or sliding pieces, with their irregular profiles, translate rotational motion into linear motion. Imagine a simple cam attached to a motor: as the cam rotates, a rod following its profile will move back and forth or up and down, animating a connected element of your sculpture. The shape of the cam dictates the precise movement, allowing for subtle oscillations or abrupt, jerky actions. Experimenting with different cam profiles opens a world of possibilities for creating complex and nuanced movements.

Cranks offer a different approach to motion control. Essentially a lever attached to a rotating shaft, a crank converts rotational motion into reciprocating linear motion. Think of the pedals on a bicycle. The circular motion of pedaling is translated into the up-and-down movement of the piston, driving the bike forward. In sculpture, cranks can be used to create rocking motions, swinging pendulums, or repetitive back-and-forth movements. Their simplicity and robustness make them ideal for various kinetic applications.

Linkages, composed of interconnected bars and pivots, provide yet another avenue for controlling motion. These systems can be incredibly complex, capable of generating intricate patterns of movement. A four-bar linkage, for example, a classic mechanism, can be configured to produce a wide range of motions, from simple rocking to more complex paths. By carefully designing the lengths and pivot points of the links, you can orchestrate specific movements, creating intricate dances of interconnected elements within your sculpture.

Ratchets and gears offer precise control over intermittent motion. A ratchet allows motion in one direction while preventing it in the other, creating a stepped or clicking movement. Combine this with a gear train, and you can achieve precise control over the timing and sequence of motions. Imagine a series of interconnected gears, each rotating at a different speed, driving a sequence of carefully timed movements within your sculpture. This level of control allows for complex, programmed sequences of motion.

Geneva drives, also known as Maltese crosses, provide a means of indexing or intermittent rotary motion. They are often used in film projectors and clockwork mechanisms to advance film or rotate hands in discrete steps. In kinetic sculpture, a Geneva drive can be used to create precise, controlled rotations, perfect for animating elements that need to move in specific increments.

Beyond these basic mechanisms, more sophisticated control can be achieved through pneumatic and hydraulic systems. These systems use compressed air or fluid to power movement, offering a different feel and dynamic than mechanical linkages. Pneumatics can create quick, powerful movements, while hydraulics offer smooth, controlled motion, often with greater force. Consider the possibilities of incorporating air cylinders or hydraulic rams into your work, using them to create expanding and contracting forms, or powerful, controlled movements.

Don't limit yourself to a single mechanism. The real magic often happens when you combine these elements. Imagine a cam controlling the speed of a crank, which in turn drives a linkage system. By layering and integrating these mechanisms, you can achieve an extraordinary level of complexity and nuance in your kinetic creations. The interplay of different movements, driven by carefully chosen mechanisms, is what brings your sculpture to life.

Remember, choosing the right mechanism depends on the specific effect you want to achieve. A gentle swaying motion might call for a simple pendulum or crank, while a complex, sequenced movement might require a combination of cams, gears, and linkages. Experiment, explore, and discover the unique expressive potential of each mechanism. Consider the materials you're working with, the scale of your sculpture, and the overall aesthetic you're aiming for. The possibilities are endless, limited only by your imagination and ingenuity.

6.2 Incorporating Motors

Electric motors offer a reliable and controllable way to introduce movement into your kinetic sculptures. From simple rotations to complex, programmed sequences, understanding the different types of motors available and how to integrate them into your work opens a world of creative possibilities. Consider the scale and weight of your sculpture. A small mobile might only need a tiny, low-torque motor, while a large, outdoor installation could require a more robust, high-torque option. Think, too, about the speed and rhythm of the intended movement. A slow, deliberate rotation calls for a different motor than a rapid, oscillating motion.

DC motors, readily available and relatively inexpensive, offer a good starting point. These motors provide a continuous rotational force and are easily controlled with variable speed controllers. Experiment with different voltages to fine-tune the speed and power output. A simple potentiometer allows for manual adjustment, giving you direct control over the motion. For more complex control, consider using a microcontroller. These small computers allow you to program specific movement sequences, timed intervals, and even responses to external stimuli like light or sound.

Stepper motors offer precise control over rotational position. Unlike DC motors, which rotate continuously, stepper motors move in discrete steps. This makes them ideal for applications requiring precise positioning or synchronized movement. Imagine a sculpture where elements need to align perfectly at certain intervals or where multiple motors need to work together in a coordinated dance. Stepper motors, controlled by a microcontroller, can achieve this level of precision.

AC motors, commonly found in household appliances, are generally more powerful than DC motors but are also more complex to control. They are best suited for larger kinetic sculptures that require significant torque to move heavy components. Incorporating an AC motor usually involves more advanced electrical work, including considerations for power supply and safety. Research and understand the specific requirements of AC motors before using them in your projects.

Regardless of the motor you choose, careful consideration must be given to its physical integration within the sculpture. The motor needs to be securely mounted and its movement effectively transferred to the desired components. Gears, pulleys, belts, and linkages are common mechanisms used to transmit and modify motion. Experiment with different combinations to achieve the desired effect. A gear train can increase torque while reducing speed, while a system of pulleys can change the direction of motion. Consider the visual impact of these mechanisms as well. Sometimes, leaving gears or linkages exposed can add to the aesthetic appeal of the sculpture, revealing the inner workings of the piece.

Power supply is another crucial aspect of incorporating motors. Batteries offer portability and simplicity, especially for smaller sculptures. Consider the battery life and accessibility for replacement. Rechargeable batteries are a sustainable option, but ensure they provide sufficient power for your motor. For larger installations, a mains power supply might be necessary. This involves working with higher voltages and requires adherence to safety regulations. Consult with a qualified electrician if you are unsure about any aspect of electrical wiring.

Finally, always prioritize safety. Working with electricity and moving parts requires careful attention to detail. Ensure all wiring is properly insulated and secured. Moving components should be designed to avoid pinching or trapping fingers or other objects. Test your sculpture thoroughly in a controlled environment before displaying it publicly. Consider incorporating safety features like emergency stops or sensors to prevent accidents. By understanding the principles of motion control and carefully planning the integration of motors, you can bring your kinetic sculptures to life, creating dynamic and engaging works of art.

6.3 Kinetic Art in Public Spaces

Public spaces offer a unique and challenging environment for kinetic art. The interplay between artwork and audience takes on a new dimension when the artwork itself is dynamic and interacts with its surroundings. Consider the scale of the space. A large plaza requires a sculpture with significant presence, while a smaller, more intimate area might suit a subtler piece. Think about sightlines and how viewers will approach and interact with the work. Will they walk around it, view it from a distance, or even touch it? These considerations will inform your design choices regarding size, movement, and materials. The environment itself plays a crucial role. Wind, rain, and even sunlight can affect the sculpture's movement and longevity. Materials must be chosen with durability in mind, able to withstand the elements and potential interactions with the public. Stainless steel, weather-resistant woods, and durable coatings become essential for preserving the artwork's integrity.

Integrating a kinetic sculpture into a public space is more than just placing it there. It's about creating a dialogue between the artwork, the environment, and the people who inhabit that space. Consider the existing architecture and landscape. Does the sculpture complement or contrast with its surroundings? How does its movement interact with the natural flow of pedestrian traffic? A well-integrated piece enhances the space, adding a layer of dynamic interest that draws people in. The context of the public space should also inform the design. Is it a park, a transportation hub, or a civic center? The function of the space and the type of people who frequent it can influence the theme and message of the sculpture. A playful, interactive piece might be suitable for a children's playground, while a more contemplative work might be appropriate for a memorial garden.

The permitting process for installing public art can be complex and varies significantly depending on location. Research local regulations early in the planning stages. You'll likely need to submit detailed proposals, including drawings, engineering specifications, and sometimes even environmental impact assessments. Engage with local authorities and community groups to ensure your project aligns with their vision for the space. This collaborative approach can not only smooth the permitting process but also foster a sense of ownership and appreciation for the artwork within the community. Safety is paramount when installing kinetic art in public spaces. Rigorous engineering and structural calculations are necessary to ensure the stability of the sculpture, especially in areas with high winds or seismic activity. Moving parts must be designed to prevent accidental injury to passersby. Regular maintenance and inspections are essential to address wear and tear and ensure the sculpture remains safe and functional over time.

The choice of driving mechanism significantly impacts the sculpture's movement and overall effect. Simple mechanisms like wind-activated spinners or gravity-driven pendulums can create elegant and organic movements. For more complex and controlled movements, motorized systems offer greater precision and the ability to program specific sequences. However, motorized systems require power sources and ongoing maintenance. Consider the accessibility of electricity and the long-term costs associated with powering the sculpture. The interplay of light and shadow adds another layer of dynamism to kinetic art. Sunlight can create dramatic shifts in appearance throughout the day, highlighting different facets of the sculpture and casting moving shadows on the surrounding environment. Artificial lighting can further enhance the artwork at night, transforming it into a focal point and extending its presence beyond daylight hours. Explore the use of reflective materials, translucent surfaces, or even integrated lighting within the sculpture itself to create captivating visual effects.

Documentation is vital for preserving the artistic intent and technical details of your work. Thorough photographs and videos of the installation process, along with detailed drawings and specifications, provide a valuable record for future maintenance, restoration, or even replication. This documentation also serves as a testament to your artistic process and can be shared with the public to deepen their understanding and appreciation of the artwork. Public art is inherently exposed to the elements and potential vandalism. Choosing durable materials is the first line of defense. Protective coatings and regular cleaning can help mitigate the effects of weathering and graffiti. Consider incorporating security measures, such as surveillance cameras or motion sensors, to deter vandalism and protect the investment in the artwork. Engaging the local community in the care and stewardship of the sculpture can also foster a sense of shared responsibility and help prevent damage.

The interaction between a kinetic sculpture and its public audience creates a unique dynamic. Consider incorporating interactive elements that allow viewers to engage with the artwork directly, perhaps by influencing its movement or triggering sound or light displays. This participatory aspect can deepen the audience's connection to the piece and transform it from a passive observation to an active experience. The kinetic nature of the artwork invites viewers to contemplate the interplay of forces and the passage of time. The ever-changing patterns of movement and light create a sense of wonder and invite reflection on the dynamic nature of the world around us. By carefully considering the context, environment, and audience engagement, kinetic sculptors can create truly transformative experiences in public spaces.

6.4 Installation and Display

The culmination of your kinetic sculpture journey lies not just in its creation, but in its presentation to the world. A thoughtfully installed piece can dramatically enhance its impact, transforming a simple mechanism into a captivating experience. Consider your sculpture's interaction with its environment. Is it designed for an indoor gallery setting, an outdoor public space, or perhaps a private collection? This context should inform your installation approach.

Indoor installations offer controlled environments, allowing for precise lighting and a more intimate viewing experience. Track lighting can highlight specific elements of your sculpture, emphasizing its movement and form. Neutral wall colors often provide an ideal backdrop, allowing the artwork to take center stage. However, a bold color choice can create a dramatic contrast, amplifying the sculpture's presence. The size and scale of the gallery space itself are important factors. A large, open space can accommodate larger, more ambitious pieces, while a smaller gallery might necessitate a more compact design. Consider the viewing distance and angles, ensuring the sculpture is visible and engaging from various perspectives. Think about how viewers will circulate around the piece and how this movement might interact with the sculpture's own motion.

Outdoor installations present a unique set of challenges and opportunities. Weather resistance becomes paramount. Protective coatings for metal components and durable wood treatments are essential. Sunlight, wind, and rain can all impact the longevity of your sculpture. Consider the surrounding landscape and how your piece integrates with it. A kinetic sculpture placed in a garden, for instance, might harness the wind to create gentle, organic movement. In a bustling urban environment, the sculpture might contrast with the static architecture, injecting a sense of dynamic energy. Public safety must also be considered. Securely anchoring the sculpture is crucial, especially in areas with high foot traffic or potential exposure to strong winds. Regular maintenance and inspections should be planned for to ensure ongoing structural integrity.

Private collections offer more flexibility in terms of installation. Collaboration with the collector is key to understanding their vision and the intended display space. Factors like lighting, surrounding décor, and the collector's personal aesthetic preferences should be considered. The sculpture's size and scale must be appropriate for the designated area, ensuring it harmonizes with the existing environment. The installation process might involve customized mounting systems or pedestals to showcase the piece effectively. Open communication and collaboration with the collector throughout the installation process are vital for a successful outcome.

Display considerations extend beyond the physical placement of your sculpture. Think about how the lighting affects the viewer's perception. Natural light can create shifting shadows and highlights throughout the day, adding another layer of dynamism to the artwork. Artificial lighting allows for greater control, emphasizing specific details and creating dramatic effects. Consider using spotlights to highlight the movement of individual components, or soft, diffused lighting to create a more ethereal atmosphere. Experiment with different lighting techniques to discover what best enhances your sculpture's visual impact.

Documentation and preservation are crucial steps in completing your kinetic sculpture project. High-quality photographs and videos are essential for showcasing your work and documenting its movement. Capture the sculpture from various angles and under different lighting conditions to fully represent its dynamic nature. Detailed written documentation should accompany the visual record. This should include a description of the materials used, the mechanisms employed, and the artistic intent behind the work. Installation instructions, maintenance procedures, and any special considerations for the sculpture's operation should also be documented. This information is invaluable for future exhibitions, preservation efforts, and for anyone who interacts with your sculpture in the future. Preservation involves actively protecting your sculpture from deterioration and damage. This includes regular cleaning, applying protective coatings, and addressing any mechanical wear and tear. For outdoor installations, weatherproofing is especially critical. Consult with conservation professionals for advice on appropriate preservation techniques for specific materials and environments. Careful documentation and meticulous preservation ensure that your kinetic sculpture will continue to captivate audiences for years to come. These final steps complete the cycle of creation, allowing your dynamic artwork to endure as a testament to your artistic vision and technical skill. By considering these aspects of installation and display, you can transform your kinetic sculpture into a truly immersive and engaging experience, bringing your artistic vision to life and sharing it with the world.

6.5 Documentation and Preservation

The longevity of your kinetic sculpture, whether crafted from metal or wood, relies heavily on thoughtful documentation and careful preservation. This isn't simply about archiving your work; it's about ensuring its continued functionality, protecting it from the ravages of time and environment, and providing valuable insight for future repairs, restorations, or even replications. A well-documented sculpture becomes more than just an object – it transforms into a living testament to your artistic process.

Begin your documentation process during the design phase. Sketch your initial concepts, noting the materials, mechanisms, and intended movements. As your design evolves, document any changes, including material substitutions or adjustments to the mechanism. These early records offer a window into your creative thinking and can be invaluable if you ever need to revisit the sculpture's original intent.

As you build your sculpture, meticulously photograph each step. Close-up images of joinery, mechanisms, and internal structures are especially important. These visual records serve as a roadmap of your construction process, simplifying future repairs or adjustments. Supplement these photos with written descriptions. Note specific hardware used, the type and quantity of adhesives, and any unique construction techniques employed. This detailed record is particularly useful for complex mechanisms, where a single misplaced component can disrupt the entire system.

Consider creating detailed diagrams, especially for intricate mechanisms or complex balancing systems. These schematics can offer a clearer understanding of the sculpture's internal workings than photographs alone. Exploded diagrams, which show the individual components separated but in their relative positions, can be particularly helpful for illustrating assembly and disassembly procedures.

For kinetic sculptures incorporating motors or electronics, include wiring diagrams and specifications for all components. Document the type of motor, its power rating, and any specific control systems used. This information is critical for troubleshooting malfunctions or replacing obsolete parts. If you use custom-programmed microcontrollers, include the code and any relevant documentation explaining its function.

Once the sculpture is complete, create a comprehensive "owner's manual." This document should consolidate all the information gathered throughout the process, from initial sketches to final assembly diagrams. It should also include instructions for installation, operation, and maintenance. Specify the ideal environmental conditions for the sculpture, including temperature and humidity ranges. Outline a regular maintenance schedule, including lubrication points, cleaning procedures, and any necessary adjustments.

Preserving your kinetic sculpture requires a proactive approach. Metal sculptures, especially those exposed to the elements, are susceptible to corrosion. Apply protective coatings, such as clear sealants or specialized metal paints, to shield the metal from moisture and air pollutants. Regularly inspect the sculpture for signs of rust or other damage, and address any issues promptly. For wooden sculptures, apply appropriate finishes to protect the wood from moisture, insects, and UV damage.

The environment in which you display your sculpture plays a significant role in its preservation. Indoor sculptures should be kept in a climate-controlled environment, away from direct sunlight and excessive humidity. Outdoor sculptures require more robust protection. Consider using weather-resistant materials and coatings, and provide adequate drainage to prevent water accumulation. If possible, design the sculpture to be easily disassembled for storage or transport during inclement weather.

Document any repairs or modifications made to the sculpture throughout its lifespan. Note the date of the repair, the nature of the problem, and the solution implemented. This ongoing documentation ensures that the sculpture's history is preserved, adding to its value and providing valuable insights for future caretakers.

Finally, consider the long-term preservation of your documentation. Digital files should be backed up regularly and stored in multiple locations to prevent data loss. Physical documents, such as sketches and diagrams, should be stored in archival-quality sleeves or folders, away from direct sunlight and moisture. By meticulously documenting and diligently preserving your kinetic sculptures, you are not just safeguarding your own artistic legacy – you are contributing to the broader understanding and appreciation of this dynamic art form. Your careful efforts ensure that these captivating creations continue to inspire and engage audiences for generations to come.

7 Chapter 7: Inspiration and Exploration

The world of kinetic sculpture is rich with ingenuity and artistic expression. From the delicate, wind-driven mobiles of Alexander Calder to the monumental, mechanically complex works of Theo Jansen, inspiration abounds. Calder's work, often characterized by brightly colored abstract shapes suspended in perfect equilibrium, demonstrates the beauty of simple, harmonious movement. His mobiles, seemingly weightless and effortless in their dance, are a testament to his mastery of balance and form. Jansen's Strandbeests, on the other hand, are a marvel of engineering and imagination. These massive, wind-powered creatures roam the beaches of the Netherlands, blurring the lines between art, science, and nature. Exploring their intricate leg mechanisms and the mesmerizing motion they create reveals a deep understanding of mechanics and a profound connection with the natural world.

These artists, along with many others, offer a glimpse into the vast potential of kinetic sculpture. Jean Tinguely's chaotic, self-destructing machines challenge the conventional notions of art and permanence, introducing an element of performance and unpredictability. George Rickey's precisely balanced, geometric forms explore the subtle interplay of gravity and movement, creating an almost meditative experience for the viewer. By studying their work, not just visually but also by researching their methods and philosophies, we can begin to understand the diverse approaches to kinetic art and the myriad ways in which motion can be expressed. Consider researching the artists mentioned here and others who resonate with you. Deep dives into their biographies, artistic statements, and the context of their work can provide invaluable insights into their creative processes and motivations.

Finding your own unique style within kinetic art is a journey of exploration and experimentation. It's about discovering what fascinates you, what kind of movement speaks to your soul, and what materials resonate with your vision. Do you find yourself drawn to the organic flow of natural forms or the precise geometry of mechanical systems? Are you captivated by the interplay of light and shadow, or the raw power of industrial materials? These questions are the starting point for your artistic journey. Begin by exploring different materials - metal, wood, plastic, found objects - and experimenting with various methods of creating motion. Try simple mechanisms like levers, pulleys, and pendulums to understand their fundamental principles.

Don't be afraid to break the rules and challenge conventional approaches. Kinetic art is a dynamic and evolving field, constantly pushing the boundaries of artistic expression. Perhaps you're drawn to the interplay of light and movement, exploring how shadows can become an integral part of your sculpture. Maybe you're interested in incorporating sound or interactive elements, engaging the viewer in a multi-sensory experience. The possibilities are endless. Embrace the unexpected, the happy accidents, and the moments of serendipitous discovery that often lead to the most innovative and exciting work. Keep a sketchbook dedicated to your kinetic art ideas. Jot down concepts, sketch potential designs, and document your experiments. This visual journal will become a valuable resource, capturing your evolving style and providing a springboard for future projects.

Developing your style is not just about the technical aspects of creating motion. It's also about finding your own unique voice, your own way of expressing yourself through movement. What stories do you want to tell with your sculptures? What emotions do you want to evoke? Think about the themes that resonate with you – nature, technology, human relationships, social commentary – and how you can explore these themes through the language of motion. Perhaps you're interested in exploring the cyclical nature of life and death through a sculpture that continuously repeats a specific movement. Or maybe you want to express the frenetic energy of a bustling city through a complex interplay of gears and levers. The key is to find a way to connect your inner world with the physical world through the dynamic medium of kinetic art.

As you experiment and explore, remember that there is no right or wrong way to create kinetic art. Your style will evolve organically over time, shaped by your experiences, influences, and discoveries. Embrace the process, be patient with yourself, and allow your creativity to guide you. Visit museums and galleries, attend art exhibitions, and connect with other kinetic artists. Engage in dialogue, share your work, and seek feedback. The exchange of ideas and perspectives can be incredibly enriching, sparking new inspirations and pushing you to explore new directions. Most importantly, keep creating, keep exploring, and keep pushing the boundaries of your own artistic potential. The world of kinetic art is waiting to be discovered, and your unique voice has the power to add something truly special to its ongoing evolution.

7.1 Kinetic Artists and Their Work

The world of kinetic art is rich with ingenuity, a testament to the human fascination with imbuing static forms with dynamic life. Exploring the works of established kinetic artists offers a powerful lens through which to understand the possibilities of this medium. Consider the whimsical, often monumental works of Alexander Calder. His mobiles, delicately balanced and responsive to air currents, epitomize the graceful interplay of form, movement, and balance. Calder's work often incorporates brightly colored abstract shapes, creating a sense of playful dynamism that engages the viewer in a delightful dance of shifting perspectives. His legacy continues to inspire artists exploring the potential of air and balance in kinetic expression.

Then there's George Rickey, whose precisely engineered sculptures harness the subtle power of wind to create mesmerizing, almost hypnotic movements. Rickey's work is characterized by its elegant simplicity and meticulous attention to detail. He favored geometric forms, often using highly polished stainless steel, which reflects the surrounding environment and adds another layer of visual complexity to the artwork's interaction with light and space. His pieces demonstrate the power of minimalist aesthetics in conveying intricate motion. His exploration of subtle shifts and delicate balances has deeply influenced subsequent generations of kinetic sculptors.

Jean Tinguely's approach stands in stark contrast, embracing chaos and humor in his complex, often self-destructing machines. Tinguely's work is a playful critique of industrial society, using found objects and discarded machinery to create dynamic sculptures that often perform absurd and unexpected actions. His metamechanic reliefs and chaotic assemblages challenge conventional notions of art and functionality, inviting viewers to question the very nature of creation and destruction. He introduced an element of the unexpected, highlighting the potential for kinetic art to be not only beautiful but also thought-provoking and even subversive.

Shifting gears from the large-scale to the intricate, Theo Jansen's Strandbeests, wind-powered creatures crafted from PVC pipes, roam the beaches like fantastical beasts from another world. Jansen's creations blur the line between art and engineering, demonstrating a deep understanding of biomechanics and a remarkable ability to harness natural forces. His Strandbeests are a testament to the power of imagination and innovation, inspiring artists and engineers alike to explore new possibilities at the intersection of art and technology. They evoke a sense of wonder and possibility, reminding us of the power of art to create entirely new forms of life.

Turning to a different application of kinetic principles, consider the mesmerizing water sculptures of Rebecca Horn. Her kinetic installations often incorporate water, light, and mechanical elements to create immersive sensory experiences. Horn's work explores themes of transformation and the human body, often using fluid, organic forms that contrast with the precision and rigidity of more traditional kinetic sculptures. Her work demonstrates the versatility of kinetic art, showcasing its potential to engage multiple senses and create evocative, emotionally resonant experiences.

These artists represent just a fraction of the rich tapestry of kinetic art. From the playful mobiles of Calder to the complex machines of Tinguely, each artist offers a unique perspective on the possibilities of movement, balance, and form. Studying their approaches, materials, and underlying philosophies can provide invaluable insights for aspiring kinetic sculptors.

Don't limit your exploration to well-known figures. Seek out emerging artists pushing the boundaries of the medium, experimenting with new materials and technologies. Visit galleries, museums, and online platforms dedicated to kinetic art. Immerse yourself in the vibrant world of moving sculpture, and let the ingenuity of others spark your own creative journey. Analyze their techniques, the materials they choose, and how they incorporate natural forces or mechanical elements into their work. Consider how they address the fundamental principles of balance, motion, and visual harmony.

Ultimately, finding your own style within kinetic art is a process of exploration and experimentation. It's about discovering what excites you, what challenges you, and what resonates with your unique artistic vision. By engaging with the work of other artists, you can gain a deeper understanding of the possibilities of the medium and develop a richer vocabulary for expressing your own ideas. Let the inspiration you draw from these masters fuel your own explorations, propelling you to create kinetic sculptures that reflect your individual perspective and contribute to the ever-evolving landscape of this dynamic art form. Remember, the journey of artistic discovery is ongoing, and the world of kinetic art is a vast and exciting playground waiting to be explored.

7.2 Finding Your Style

Your journey as a kinetic sculptor involves a continuous interplay between material, motion, and your unique perspective. Discovering your style is not a destination but an evolving process of experimentation and self-discovery. It's about understanding your inherent inclinations and allowing them to manifest in the rhythmic dance of metal and wood. Consider this chapter a compass, guiding you through the exciting terrain of artistic expression.

Begin by examining your responses to the world around you. What captures your attention? Are you drawn to the graceful sway of branches in the wind, the rhythmic crashing of waves, or the intricate mechanisms of a clock? These observations, seemingly mundane, hold the seeds of your artistic language. Document these moments, sketch them, write about them. This practice cultivates a deeper awareness of your aesthetic preferences, laying the foundation for a distinctive style.

Next, consider the materials themselves. Do you feel a stronger connection to the cool, industrial feel of metal, or the warm, organic nature of wood? Each material possesses unique characteristics that lend themselves to different forms of expression. Metal, with its strength and rigidity, can be coaxed into precise, geometric forms, allowing for intricate mechanisms and controlled movements. Wood, with its inherent warmth and flexibility, invites exploration of organic shapes and flowing, natural movements. Experiment with both mediums, pushing their boundaries and discovering the nuances of each. This hands-on exploration will reveal which material resonates most deeply with your artistic vision.

Don't be afraid to break the rules. While understanding the fundamental principles of kinetic sculpture is crucial, true originality often arises from challenging conventions. Experiment with unconventional materials, explore unexpected combinations of motion, and push the boundaries of balance and form. Perhaps you'll discover a novel way to incorporate light, sound, or even interactive elements into your work. These explorations, even if they initially seem unconventional, can lead to breakthroughs in your artistic style.

Study the masters, but don't imitate them. Immerse yourself in the world of kinetic art. Explore the works of Alexander Calder, George Rickey, and Theo Jansen. Analyze their techniques, their use of materials, and the emotions their sculptures evoke. However, resist the urge to simply replicate their styles. Instead, use their work as a springboard for your own creativity. Ask yourself: what resonates with me about this piece? What can I learn from it, and how can I apply those principles in a way that is uniquely my own?

Your style is also an extension of your personal narrative. What stories do you want to tell through your art? What emotions do you want to evoke in your viewers? Kinetic sculpture, with its inherent dynamism, offers a powerful platform for expressing complex themes and narratives. Perhaps you're fascinated by the cyclical nature of time, the delicate balance of ecosystems, or the intricate dance of human relationships. Allow these themes to inform your design choices, shaping the movement, form, and materials of your sculptures.

Embrace the iterative process. Finding your style is not a linear journey. It's a continuous cycle of experimentation, reflection, and refinement. Don't be discouraged by initial setbacks or failed experiments. Each attempt, whether successful or not, provides valuable insights into your artistic process. Embrace these "failures" as opportunities for growth, and allow them to inform your future endeavors. Keep a sketchbook or journal to document your ideas, experiments, and reflections. This record will serve as a valuable tool for tracking your progress and identifying emerging patterns in your work.

Finally, remember that your style is not static. It will continue to evolve as you grow as an artist. Embrace this evolution, allowing your experiences, influences, and insights to shape your artistic vision. The most compelling artistic styles are those that are authentic and reflective of the artist's unique perspective. Trust your instincts, embrace the journey, and allow your individual voice to resonate through the dynamic language of kinetic sculpture. The kinetic sculptor's playground is yours to explore. Embrace the challenge, and allow your unique style to emerge from the interplay of material, motion, and your own creative spirit.

www.ingramcontent.com/pod-product-compliance
Ingram Content Group UK Ltd.
Pitfield, Milton Keynes, MK11 3LW, UK
UKHW021437240125
4283UKWH00041B/640

9 798348 406844